West Coast Journey – California ar

During the summer of 2010, I went

was so much speculation in the months leading up to our departure as

to whether I would go, but it was for my dad's 50th birthday so I knew I

would. Right up until we left there was emotions flying high about how

it was going to be with us on a family holiday for the first time in years.

Mum, Dad, Hannah and I. But I can honestly say, I wouldn't change it for

anything. What first started off as some A5 notes has become this

massive project, and I hope it is as enjoyable to read as it was to both

write and experience.

Day One – August 18th

Today was a travelling day, and that's all it was. It doesn't count as the first day of the trip because all we achieved was getting from one continent to the other safely, though it's fair to say it contained lots of stress and emotion. There were many things about today which bothered me, the packing up and leaving and being isolated from my home life and my boyfriend, and knowing I'd be spending the whole day stuck on a plane. But the excitement was there too, as California is somewhere I've always wanted to go. It's always all over the television and it's the pinnacle of celebrity culture, and we were going there, now.

We spent the early morning bustling about and throwing last minute and probably unnecessary items into already bulging suitcases. The wheels were each making small figures of eight as they rolled dramatically out to the awaiting taxi before it was hoisted up our steps and into the boot. It was the first of the many upcoming trips it would be facing over the next few weeks.

Beginning the day with an early wake up call, I was and using vacuum bags to make it look like I'd packed less. We were at Newport train station before I was fully awake.

As the taxi drove up to the end of our cul-de-sac to turn around, the boot already shut and Hannah, Mum and I in our seats Dad stopped the car.

"I don't think I've shut the bathroom window."

"Oh for goodness sake. Go on, quick hurry." Mum was annoyed. "Check the back door whilst you're at it!" He waved back acknowledging her remark. Mum smiled embarrassed at the driver.

We were thrown out onto the side of the road by the extremely cheery taxi driver with silver hair; he was eager to please and took an interest in where we were going. He wished us a pleasant trip before disappearing into the city traffic.

Stopping in the sundrenched lobby whilst Mum hunted for our tickets, Hannah and I pulled our cases around in a circle on the bumpy tiled floor. It really was an ugly station, the floor was like that of a swimming pool changing room and the staff weren't exactly cheery. Then the hard part; trying to drag our suitcases up the stairs to the correct platform. Mum couldn't lift her case, grappling with it as we all ran ahead for the train.

"Come on Anne!"

As we all hurried on, she accepted the help of a stranger, and not a bad looking one either. We are one of those families that make everything by the skin of their teeth and to which problems always seem to arise. We were always meant to get on that train as the man drew the whistle to his lips. For example, today, when we got on that train to London, before we had even boarded Dad had left one of his bags on the platform.

"Where's my bag?"

"Excuse me?"

"My blue bag?" Dad was getting impatient as more people piled into the gangway, squishing us further down and away from the door.

"I've only got enough hands for my own."

A quick glance out of the window revealed it slumped against a railing. Suddenly the whistle blew for the final time.

"Go and get it then," he nudged Mum. "Quickly."

She tutted in disbelief, and she dropped everything to run back to get it. Making it back with seconds to spare. Out of breath, she threw it into his arms and shot him a look.

The fate of the day really began there.

"Why didn't you grab it in the first place?!?" He always tries making it someone else's fault.

"It's *your* bag, that's down to you!"

The tiff lasted a few minutes into the journey before fizzling out. Here we go, Hannah and I rolled our eyes. It quickly became something to laugh about as it usually does, a 'could only happen to us' moment. The Newport skyline slowly vanished, and so did the negativity.

Once in London, we boarded another train to Heathrow airport, the Heathrow Express. This one had a television and internet access, not that either of them were any good. The TV was mostly talking about the train and its features, and what we would be passing through. Boring.

The confusion of the checking in process began. The luggage had to be gone; the boarding passes ready, and off to the departure lounge and ready to go all in a matter of minutes. The staff wants you there and settled early, but once you are there's bugger all to do.

Trying to kill time I went in search of food. Not a cat in hell's chance of me eating a plane meal, no matter how much the hunger pains made themselves known. The smell always makes me feel ill, and their appearance is yet to win me over, so I think I'll stick to taking on my snacks. There's something about food sealed in silver trays whilst hot that makes me gag. I can't describe it, the feeling of unleashing a trapped smell, I can't even pick at the rest of the tray. I hate having it near me, yet every year Mum insists on paying extra for one.

"It's a long flight, you need to eat something."

I'd much rather buy a nice hot snack beforehand that will tide me over until some decent food comes along. It becomes a guessing game, when you'll next eat. So hungry you feel sick. But give me that any day over plane food swirling inside me.

Eleven hours was the flight time to Los Angeles and even with the overpowering hunger pains that kicked in after a while the flight went very smoothly. Although, I don't think eleven hours on a plane can ever go quickly, no matter how much entertainment you have. Especially when you have a very excitable child sat next to you, the constant prodding and movement soon gets tedious.

"Julia, look what's on."

"Yes Hannah."

"Julia play Who Wants to be a Millionaire."

"No Hannah."

"Pass me my bag?"

"Oh for God's sake."

I flicked between films, games and music albums on the television in front of me, trying to ignore the restless head it was attached too. Then

I tried to get some sleep in the upright blue chairs that refuse to go back, and if they do you risk hitting the person behind, which always proves difficult.

LAX Airport, different story entirely. The first thing you want to do after travelling is rest and above all sleep. Even if you are one of those people, like me, who can sleep anywhere, you never feel rested after flying. It didn't happen. I always feel dirty after flying, groggy and not in the mood for anything. So I didn't enjoy being met by horrendous queues, a chaotic and unorganised set up, which meant the process took much longer than necessary. They are so suspicious of everybody, glaring at you making you feel like a criminal. Your body clock is all over the place and you have this to deal with, being eight hours behind really messes with your head.

Finding the luggage was a mission in itself, as people were just lugging bags off the carousel, and then abandoning them on the floor when they realised it wasn't theirs. None of our luggage came out and the carousel became empty, we soon became the only people stood there.

Dad consulted a nearby staff member who told us to check on the floor, as this happens a lot by the sounds of it. Dad and I each went around the belt a different way, and found all of our bags strewn in various directions by passengers who thought it belonged to them. Very insensitive. There was even a queue to get out of the airport, so Mum joined it whilst we were on a bag hunt, and was almost at the front when we reappeared.

"Where do we go now?"

"Straight out through that door, sir."

It should have been that simple. Mum jumped out of the queue and followed Dad as he strode off into the distance.

"Where are you going sir?!?"

"We were told to go through here."

"There's a line, get to the back."

"Right."Dad cursed under his breath before turning to Mum. "Straight through there he said, this is a joke." The bad mood reappeared as we trudged back to the snaking queue.

After eventually getting out and finding a cab, the crowds began to die down as we made our way to downtown Hollywood. By now it was getting late and becoming rather dark. The city was lit up as we passed through the iconic scenery, but seemed a lot scarier when we got to the Walk of Fame. A car of young boys pulled up alongside our cab and started trying to talk to me, their car bouncing to the beat of their music. I really wasn't in the mood for this. Luckily they went a different way as we turned into the car park of the Hollywood Heights hotel alongside the Walk of Fame.

Getting a McDonald's late at night in Hollywood was one of the weirdest experiences I have ever encountered. Surrounded by drug addicts, it is not a safe place to be, not the classy Hollywood image that everyone believes it to be. It's more of a dark place than the news lets on, the side where celebrities take overdoses in gutters and party in rough neighbourhoods. Instead of a celebrity style walkway fit for the stars, late at night it's teenagers that litter the sidewalk. After walking for just a few minutes a woman was asking me for change, she was drugged up to the eyeballs. It was written all over her drained face as she held out her hands, desperate for her next fix. Gangs surrounded the one half of the Walk, bottles in hand, jeering and fighting in baggy jeans and oversized baseball caps, watching your every move as you entered their territory. There were no police in sight, so the Walk remained dirty and with rubbish strewn everywhere. All dimly lit on the unvisited side of the road where the streetlights didn't reach. That's where gangs were lurking all around, down alleyways and slumped on the ground outside restaurants. There was also a homeless woman sleeping on the side of the main road on a busy walkway, un-fazed by the bustle going on around her. She had so much stuff with her, a few bags and a mattress, complete with a blanket and some kind of pillow.

The McDonald's itself was packed, the menu seemed different and I had no idea what I wanted. Being truthful, I was too tired to care, but I needed to eat something. Everything Dad and I ordered came back twice the size it would have at home, but I was starving. It had been hours since I last had anything, it was on British soil in fact. We carried it back to the hotel through busy streets, and not a friendly busy. At home, I'd have been terrified by the sight I saw before me, but after

nineteen hours of travelling, there's not a lot more that can affect you.

Day Two – August 19th

Today was a rather busy day. We all woke up mummified in sheets that had become untucked in the night. Hannah was fanned out next to me, her hair masking her face as she slept, making the piece on her nose blow gently up and down. She was facing me, starting to stir. She always could get comfortable anywhere. After a sleepless and very stuffy night where Dad couldn't figure out the air conditioning, we left the hotel early.

He'd spent at least half an hour late last night bashing the vent by the window. "How the hell does this work now? This is stupid."

It was late and nobody really cared about the air con, even though it was like a sauna. It was blowing feebly; me breathing would have had more of an impact.

"It is doing something," Mum said.

"A lot of good that'll be to those sleeping on the other side of the room."

Mum shrugged. She couldn't be bothered for it, Hannah and I were stretched out and that's what she wanted to be doing. He wasn't going to leave it though, she knew that for nothing.

"Ah Ha!"

Out of nowhere cold air hit my face as I lay on the far side of the room, finally some of the heat was gone and it was cool enough to sleep.

We were eager to get started, and to go and experience the heat and the famous sights for the first time. Breakfast. A small buffet like you would expect at a Holiday Inn, a few silver trays with lids and a cereal station. Decorated mainly with wood and lime seating, our table was by the window. It was rather busy and there was queue for the hot food. Although it was early, the sun was already streaking the floorboards and the traffic was starting to build. A few minutes gazing outside and the food gone, we were off.

Now it was time to set about exploring the sites of LA, starting with some shopping. The whole walkway was packed with people and cameras, so at first it was pretty impossible to get anywhere. It was easier to start with the souvenir shops situated along the Walk of Fame itself, picking up touristy bits to take home and keep, and presents to give, whilst grabbing every chance possible to sit and take a picture with a Hollywood star. The same shop seemed to be duplicated all the way down the road as each shop sells pretty much the same bits, but some tend to have more and at better prices. Once you've been in one souvenir shop though you've been in them all. As much as you tell yourself that though you still go in almost every single one. It did start to get tedious eventually, and we ditched the stupid caps and plastic Oscars to get out and do something. It was Hollywood after all.

We ventured along the Walk for a while, taking it in and walking up and down a few times to make sure we saw everything. We were tourists on the first day of our holiday; we stood out a mile off, gawping at everything in sight with cameras permanently pressed to our noses. I ended up capturing over one hundred photographs over the course of that first day. We bumped into a few odd characters in celebrity costumes offering photographs, such as Johnny Depp lookalikes and others who just hoped they looked the part; they expected money for their troubles, unlikely. There were a lot of sales reps constantly flocking around you, grabbing you when you took a breather from the heat. Each of the hundreds of tourists added to the experience of this exciting place. Many tour guides were trying to flog their tours to the public, such as open bus tours, rentals and a few out of town experiences. Had it not been for the money, I think I would gladly have been booked on everything. Walking along we were approached by a nice and informative tour guide, and by midday we were booked onto the tour of the "Hollywood Homes."

"Two adult's two children?"

"Three adult's one child." As soon as she opened her mouth Mum knew she shouldn't have. It was going to be the beginning of a reoccurring theme we thought, so next time none of us would be correct that mistake.

"You only look fifteen," the man laughed ripping off our tickets. Hannah smirked, she was thirteen.

We walked over the bus stop after talking to the man for a few minutes. Hannah was still chuckling.

"I don't know what you're laughing at," I said, "he thought you were eight."

Before the tour began, we explored the surrounding Kodak Theatre. Outside, there are handprints left there by celebrities who have visited it over the years and left their mark in the concrete, many of those have now passed away, such as Elizabeth Taylor, John Wayne and Frank Sinatra. Outside the next door Gauman's Chinese theatre lay this huge concrete yard swarming with people trying out the handprints and footprints from the likes of Marilyn Monroe, Brad Pitt, the Olsen twins, the Harry Potter cast and many more.

Some were less recognisable, for example, Brad Pitt signed his slate "BP," so it is often overlooked by eager tourists. There are always tour guides lurking nearby to point out the small details to you, to make sure you don't overlook anything, as some of the writing isn't very readable or as easily spotted. This includes the fountain in the corner in remembrance of Marilyn Monroe and her contribution to the industry, marked with a gold plaque. As well as how tiny her footprints looked in her high heels, even though they were a respectable size six.

At 2pm the tour was ready to begin. We went back to the theatre to board the bus. The group for the afternoon were lead out through the buildings back entrance to the car park full of open topped cars. The tour got underway and we got onto the open topped "Buddy Fun Bus" (basically a larger version of a pickup truck) complete with a set of headphones each. There were nine seats in the cars, so Mum, Hannah and I had the middle row.

"I'll just sit on my own then," said Dad, and took a seat in the front row with an Israeli gay couple.

The tour guide took us, the Israeli's and some New Yorkers around Beverly Hills, Hollywood, West Hollywood and Bel-Air. The couple beside Dad each wore large baseball caps and spent most of the tour snuggling and taking photos. The New Yorkers sat at the back of the bus were very vocal, asking questions and generally speaking very loudly.

Each of them wore large sunglasses and was very similar in appearance. All were unshaven with very dark hair and clothing, and very strong New York accents. It was apparent very early on that they were going to be asking a lot of questions. For a group of men, they were very giggly.

Our tour guide was very friendly and informative about the city and its famous properties. On one of our first stops he pulled over to say:

"Here on the right is the home of Christina Aguilera, who recently purchased this property from the Osbourne family." As the move was only a recent thing it is clear the guides are very up to date with all that goes on on their routes, and are ready to answer any question they are faced with from curious tourist's day in and day out.

The different areas of LA ranged differently in price, and allowed us an insight into the lives of the rich and famous. It allowed you to see who is the most successful in what they do as it is reflected in which part of the city they live. The area of Bel-Air is the most expensive, as many of the homes we weren't able to see through security and high walls. We saw homes used in the movies, such as *Halloween* and *Nightmare on Elm Street*, which are almost identical in real life to how they appear in the films, just in a residential street and with people living there.

We saw many mansions, such as Michael Jackson's, which strangely enough is right on the main tour road. His house is clearly visible to passers-by, with almost nothing keeping prying eyes away from his private life. The window of the room in which he died was right above the road, so many paparazzi were able to be nearby when he passed away. The stop sign on the junction outside his gate is spray painted with "This is it STOP hating" a tribute to the late pop star.

Marilyn Monroe's and Simon Cowell's houses are opposite one another, though Marilyn's was more picturesque with trees and brickwork. It isn't known who lives there now but it is still very much the same on the outside and garden as when she was alive. Nature plays a very large role in the house, making it look very suburban. Whereas Simon Cowell has a bright white mansion completely modernised to his tastes and much further back from the road. Many of the houses were situated behind trees and fences, to make it seem almost accidental that you can't see the house or the grounds. In the case of Ronald

Reagan's home, security moved us on, meaning something was either happening or due any minute. As it happened, we arrived just minutes before Nancy Reagan.

We later went up to the Hollywood Hills in order to be as close as possible to the Hollywood sign and the striking view of the Los Angeles skyline. We were lucky enough to see the view on a cloudless day, with none of the regular smog to block our vision. The sight of a mass of buildings in their thousands reached miles into the distance, with traffic weaving through the giant city. The sun reflected off each of the spotless towers illuminating the millions of windows staring back at you. We learnt a lot about the city and its hotspots, and facts like the Hollywood sign reading "Hollywood Land" before the letters fell down the hill many years ago. There are around four million people living in LA spread across its enormous span, so it is impossible to get to see everything. This is why select tours are available to take you to different places of interest, but it's all about what you want to see and what you can afford to do.

"I'll take your picture folks." We hadn't been able to have one of us all, we jumped at the chance.

"That's lovely, thank you." Mum held it up for us to see, an image of a family against the skyline.

It lets you believe in films that you can go right up to the Hollywood sign, stand on the letters and walk behind them. This isn't the case, as we weren't allowed anywhere near it. I was very disappointed that my only view of it was about a mile in the distance.

After the tour we headed to the pool at the back of the hotel for a rest. The weather remained hot for the entire day, so buying a hat of some sort was essential. The pool required a key card to get out of the building and it was almost a mission to get the gate of the walkway open. People walked passed and laughed as I faffed with the glass wall preventing me from entering the pool, surely it shouldn't be this hard? I hung back until someone else entered, therefore looking less foolish and having more of an idea how this stupid contraption worked.

We sat in a cabana for a few hours before having dinner in the massive Hard Rock Cafe, a venue that sits 900 people, ready to plan the next day.

I wrote in my journal as the shade fell over the pool.

"Did you enjoy today?"

Dad was flat out and Hannah was swimming so I knew the question was aimed at me. Mum was perched on the edge of her sun bed awaiting my response.

"Yes I did, a lot. It'll take a lot to top it." We laughed. This was only the first day after all.

Day Three – August 20th

Today was our last day in Los Angeles. Tomorrow, after breakfast, we will be leaving for Las Vegas. This meant that today was the day to get everything done, and all the iconic spots visited. Well, aside from what we had checked off already. We left the hotel rather early and headed for the famous Kodak Theatre. For those who don't know, the Kodak Theatre is where the Oscars are held.

"Do you even know what the Kodak Theatre is?"

"No?"

"Didn't think so," Hannah shook her head whilst giving a smug grin. Mum laughed, seemed I was the only one who didn't know.

Inside, there were many shops as it had a sort of mall underneath; the actual venue itself was upstairs and around the back away from prying eyes. The auditorium is only open for authorised tours, and permits no photography at all.

The annoying thing about having foreign currency is carrying around ridiculous amounts of change that you can't convert back, so I bought a pair of earrings and some bits of jewellery off the stalls and some water using up ten cent and five cent pieces.

"Do you want some change?" I asked the kiosk worker, thinking she would be delighted.

"Sure OK," she smiled.

You could see she instantly regretted the decision when I emptied my purse and counted out eight dollars in shrapnel. I could barely pick it up, yet every time we go away this amount seems to follow me home. About time I used it on something. My purse could actually close, wouldn't be surprised if her till drawer didn't though. I scooped it up in my palm and presented it proudly to her. "That should be right," I smiled.

Although the tour of the building only lasted half an hour, it was very interesting and enlightening. It revealed all the tricks that go on behind the scenes, and long the actual preparation takes weeks to make everything perfect. For example, for the benefit of the TV cameras people are employed to wear suits and dresses so whenever someone leaves their seat, even just for a toilet break, they rush in to fill the spot so the venue never looks empty for the cameras. The decorations were extravagant and unique, different colour schemes are accommodated each year to make the event seem different. By setting up the tables in honour of different cultures and scenes, such as a Chinese style set-up, streamers and banners draped the hall, so on television it never looks like the same venue. There were examples of decorations gone by displayed around the corridors, as well as photographs of famous Oscar winners from decades gone by, most of which have now passed away.

After the tour, we took an open top bus tour known as the "Red Route" around Los Angeles. Hannah chose the first stop, a place called

"Millions of Milkshakes," a cafe known for being a celebrity hotspot. As we headed down the stairs of the bus to get off, my parents had already gone ahead when she ran back up the stairs.

"Where's she gone now?"

"I don't know."

Scared the bus was going to drive off with her still on it, I had to call for her loudly in front of the driver so he knew he had to wait.

"What the hell is she playing at?"

She came bolting down the stairs empty handed and got off to receive a telling off.

"What was that about?"

"My camera case fell off my lap when I stood up. I couldn't find it though."

"Jesus, Hannah." That started a rant on the sidewalk there and then. What would she have done if the bus had driven off? Etc etc.

With everyone now grumpy, we went over to the smoothie place. Inside there was a celebrity GPS system installed on the wall, telling you where celebrities had been spotted and how long ago. For example, Kim

Kardashian was spotted having lunch at a nearby restaurant ten hours ago. This place allowed celebrities to come in and make their own signature shake, and name it after themselves, as the likes of Miley Cyrus and Pamela Anderson have already done. Their pictures were displayed around the pink, yellow and purple walls holding the shakes they had produced.

After buying a milkshake, Hannah and her enormous shake sat outside on the busy Sunset Boulevard lined with palm trees and celebrity gatherings to enjoy it.

"How is it Hannah?" The answer was already apparent with how far apart the sips were and the constant stirring that was going on. "Nice?"

"Yeah."

She was struggling with it was the truth. She turned to me.

"Have some it's good." The way she was smacking her lips said otherwise.

"No thanks, it looks gross."

She turned away again. She was stuck with it, a large cup of frothy, milky liquid now stood between us and the rest of our day.

The busy four lanes of traffic were surrounded by a spotlessly clean city and freshly cut grass, and lots of flashy cars speeding up and down. A band called the "New Boyz" arrived as we were sat outside, and the shop was closed for them to make their shake. Paparazzi were lurking as they stopped outside, and people began to get turned away from the shop temporarily. The boys stood hanging around by us for ages, as if they wanted to be recognised, but we had no idea who they were. Neither did any of the other customers who turned up to the closed shop, and those who pressed their faces against the doors in the hope of spotting a celebrity were disappointed.

We left this scene behind and headed into Beverly Hills on foot. We walked through it for twenty minutes before going along Camden and Rodeo Drives. As the most expensive place to shop, the designer labels were a distant dream to the likes of us. Though it was great to see what it is like there is reality after seeing it perceived on television. The parking meters even had credit card slots in them instead of change slots, that said everything.

We walked through and went past many places and brands we had heard of and couldn't afford, and with everything there Mum was complimented on a cap she had just bought in a souvenir shop.

She smiled smugly clutching the cap. "Come on, we better go and get the bus."

To the bus stop we went and waited a while for the right bus. As great a place as it was and how it was exciting to be here, we were starting to feel a bit out of place. Though I'm positive if it were down to Hannah we would have ended up spending the whole afternoon window shopping and trying to spot celebrities. I poked around in a nearby pharmacy whilst we waited for its arrival.

Next stop was the Farmers Market, one of the most adorable places I have ever seen. Again, somewhere I didn't know anything about. Mum had done her research that's for sure. Set up with lots of little shops and stalls and also lots of well known brands, it was situated in a small village area alongside the busy LA lifestyle. It was rural and nothing like anything I had seen before, picturesque with a tiny theatre and a tram running through the middle of it. There was an inside area of stalls and canopies selling souvenirs and many types of food. A lot of it was like the many shops we had visited before, except they were squished together in a large tent. We ate at a sort of Southern style takeaway served by a scary butch Southern woman in plaits. She had a serious face but seemed nice enough.

Hannah and I started to walk around a bit, and Mum and Dad caught up when we got further towards the main shops. It was so well kept and clean everywhere, it made such a difference. Mum lifted her arm in an exaggerated point to a restaurant on the right.

"Cheesecake Factory," she smiled.

"Yeah?"

"Nothing. We went to one in Florida that's all. We'll be going to one at some point."

I nodded and humoured her as she gazed up at it. I'd never heard of it.

It was getting later now and the light of the setting sun was shining through the tents. Outside there stood a large shining clock tower on the immaculate brickwork labelled "Farmers Market," a meeting place in which to catch the tram. After a small break in the road, the brickwork continued onto the line of shops. The tram took you from one end of the market to the other, from tents to large high street shops and restaurants. All which were only a few feet away. It was very peaceful and quiet though, like being in a small village with a very enclosed community.

There was an Apple shop, and the dogs were allowed to just go inside, no tying up outside in this city.

I jumped a mile when a dog was roaming around us amongst the Ipods. It was like he was browsing with the rest of us.

"Julia, there's a dog in here..."

"Yes I can see."

"I don't think he's a guide dog."

"No he isn't, he's a pet. She isn't blind."

Confused, we stepped outside to be greeted with a dog being pulled along in a small cart and another wearing sunglasses. What a place!

Tonight, after the bus finally came to take us back, we ate in Hooters on the Walk of Fame. I bought a souvenir t-shirt whilst we waited for our table, I'd always wanted a Hooters top and the place was so busy I had plenty of time to get one.

"I'll have a men's one," I said to the waitress. "I want it to be baggy."

She smiled and handed one over, the ladies vests were a let down in terms of what I was hoping for, but I wasn't going to tell her that.

When we finally sat down my mum asked for a children's menu for Hannah.

"And here's one for you" said a smiling waitress placing one in front on me along with a handful of crayons. My dad was creasing as I looked up at her.

"Go on," he said. "Tell her how old you are."

"Umm, I'm nineteen."Her smile vanished and she scurried off almost scarlet and apologetic. Leaving our table very amused.

Through the course of the night many staff members kept walking past our table to study her mistake and have a laugh about it, I know because they weren't exactly discreet. It was a different way to leave LA so say the least, and left us in a good mood and ready to move on to the next place and the rest of the shenanigans we were bound to face.

Day Four – August 21st

Today we left Los Angeles and flew to Las Vegas. The flight was a very short one, only lasting about an hour. It was like getting on a bus, choose your own seat and away you go, a much better alternative to the five hour drive it would have been.

We left Hollywood late morning, and left LAX around 1pm. As to be expected, nothing ran smoothly, and our flight was delayed an hour. Being stuck in an airport for such a tiny journey was rather annoying, especially as I couldn't get the wifi to work and there weren't many shops about.

"Any luck with your phone?"

"No, it won't connect to anything."

"Why don't you have a look in the shops then?"

"You can hardly call these shops."

Silence.

"What about your DS?"

Ah the DS. With the game I'd paid twenty quid for in order to be able to go on the Internet whilst we were away.

"Waste of money, total crap. I don't even know what I'm supposed to do with it."

I threw both devices back into my bag as Hannah annoying surfed the web on her Ipod next to me.

An hour later we were away and flying out of California.

Arriving just after 3.30pm, we were stood in the most surreal arrival lounge I have ever seen. My family and I walked for what seemed like ages to get to the luggage carousel, through lounges of game machines and food shacks. It was clearly a priority to place them right at the boarding gates before you go anywhere near the luggage. Every possible space was filled with blazing lights bouncing off hundreds of slot machines, and the constant bleeping of winning and losing. Money was being wasted everywhere you turned, even alongside in the luggage collection and food court. Unfortunately though, after a very bumpy landing the last thing I felt like doing was sitting in a room of lights and constant pinging noises. The landing was awful.

"You've gone all green."

"Thanks Mum."

After such a quick trip I spent the last fifteen minutes of the journey sat bolt upright with my eyes shut gripping onto the seat. My breathing quickened and the view outside the window was shaking excessively.

Little did I know how many machines would now be everywhere I turned for the next few days. There wasn't a quiet area in sight so we decided to brace the smouldering heat for the first time, leaving the air conditioned airport and fruit machines behind.

Vegas is the hottest place I think I have ever experienced. Almost everywhere outside of the strip is desert, with roads running through the middle of it, I half expected to see tumble weeds rolling up and down the freeway as we made the short trip from airport to the centre of all the action. We reached Bally's hotel on the strip after only a ten rninute journey from the airport. The hotel was a huge white building around half way up the strip itself. This is amongst the more famous Planet Hollywood and Bellagio hotels. Our hotel had an archway which connected to a long escalator, as the main entrance was a huge drop off point for guests. The glass walkway was like being in a greenhouse every time you set foot out of the air conditioned hotel. Like being trapped in a hot tunnel until you reached the outside. I was totally taken aback by the scorching temperature, which lay at 105°F in the shade, a total contrast to a windy LA.

"This is ridiculous." Dad was swatting himself with a leaflet. "This really is desert heat."

Crossing through pure desert and then ending up on this downtown strip contrasted dramatically, from wide open space with nothing going on to this busy action-packed area. Everything was lit up like nothing I had ever seen before, even in the day time. There were slot machines everywhere, on streets in the walls like cash points, and even in the toilets. Our hotel was enormous, filled with casinos and people, though I suppose they all are. The entire lobby was a sea of gambling and lights, and downstairs there was a shopping mall and many restaurants to choose from. It was much more like a busy shopping centre than a hotel. There was an outdoor pool which it was just too hot to sit by, so we could only handle it for a few hours in the afternoon. It was way too exposed. We did a lap around the outside before settling on an available few sun beds in the shade. Though even there it was blistering. Even though we had only been in Vegas a few hours, it was as though the wind didn't exist.

From the low level pool, I could look up at the hotel and its thousands of rooms. We were on floor 23 situated in the North Tower, and that alone was a full hotel. The view from our window looked across at the Bellagio hotel, famous for its fountains, which were especially beautiful at night. Every night the fountains would shoot up and perform a sort of show, the water criss-crossing to dramatic music and surrounded by white lights, luckily our room gave it justice.

Starving and still taking in the hotel and our surroundings, we came across a cafe called "Nosh" in the lobby so we could have a snack to tide us over before going out to explore. This was just basically a Subway restaurant, except the portions were on a much larger scale. It was very small and convenient, but it would tide us over until it was tea time later. Dad and I ended up sharing a sub, and a portion of chips, which was enough for all four of us to share.

"Surely this isn't a small."

"It is compared to that one," I pointed to a table behind us to two men sharing what looked like a loaf of bread filled with meat and salad.

Hannah ordered a 'small' lemonade, which turned up brimming with ice, much larger than we had expected, but by this time we weren't shocked. It was filled with this crushed up ice which gave her the funniest of brain freezes. Needless to say she didn't finish it even though she was supposedly thirsty.

We spent two hours walking the strip in the dark, and still didn't reach anywhere near the end of it. After resting up and having a shower and a change of clothes, we were all ready to head out and explore, reimbursed with energy. Dad directed us left out of the hotel, leading us as far down as we could see, but there was still no sign of the strip ending anytime soon. Our feet were hurting and even late at night it was still impossibly hot and we had to keep stopping to buy water.

There was no shortage of people to buy it from as there was someone every few yards, along with the odd homeless man. It was obvious everybody needed water and people would stop anywhere to get it, so they must make a fortune. But in order to get to the water, the streets were lined with people tapping leaflets and throwing them at you, it was ridiculous. They literally lined every bit of the walkway; it was not only annoying but also really unsettling. They had leaflets offering services for late at night with pictures of naked girls, but were literally throwing them at every single passerby. Even at the likes of Hannah.

All the homeless men I saw were laughing and joking with those around them, some even having signs in front of them which read: "I'm not going to lie, I just want a beer."

"Did I read that right?"

I spun round to see my parents reading it too, trying to hold in the smirks until they had passed the man. "At least he's honest!" We walked through the hundreds of leaflet throwers to get to the other side of the road.

I suppose there are a lot worse places to be homeless in than in Las Vegas.

It was a very dry heat, and we had to keep going inside to cool down. Even going over walkways and down steps ended up being trivial because it was too hot to hold the rails, even though that wasn't immediately obvious. It was so surreal that even late at night, when it was pitch black, you couldn't hold a hand rail because it would burn you. I must have grabbed hold of a fair few rails before I got it into my head that they were scorching – Because it was night time it doesn't seem to register in your head that you can't touch it, silly really.

Hannah and I took loads of photos, more so at night, because everything was at its best. I wanted pictures of everything, every corner and every hotel, just to make sure I hadn't missed something great. It's impossible, because after a while all the lights seem to blend together and everything begins to look similar. In the air is a different story though, because it isn't all a few feet from your face blinding you, it is far enough away for you to enjoy it properly. The destination we were heading for tonight was the New York New York hotel. This one had a rollercoaster on the side of it, which she was very desperate to ride. I wasn't in the frame of mind to ride it there and then, but knew I'd regret not going on. It wrapped around the whole hotel hundreds of feet in the air, and was very picturesque from the top. It was bright red against the pale brickwork, which made it appear all the more daunting. Riding at night was a lot easier and more comfortable, as the seats were slightly more bearable to sit on. When queuing to get in to the loading bay, a woman who had ridden it a few times approached us.

"Here, have my pass. It's valid for a few hours yet." We were shocked. Not a lot of generosity like this back home.

"Thank you; let me..."

"No no honey, you take it and enjoy. I've ridden it enough for one day."

The four of us stood there smiling by a set of lockers and she walked away. Dad nodded at her as she left.

"You're sure you won't come on?" I asked them as the stood back from the crowds clutching our bags.

"Yes yes, you two go and enjoy yourselves," and they shooed us away through some metal bars to the back of the queue and where I could collect a ticket.

At $14 dollars a ticket for one ride, you can't go wrong with a freebie. It was a short and fast ride, but well worth it as it gave us a real feel for the place we were in, and it was nice to have breeze blowing on you for a change even if you are upside down. The climb to the top was steep and we didn't really know what to expect. Hannah was chatting away as we made our way higher and higher, and then suddenly her words turned to squeals as we plummeted downwards and upside down. It made me quite sad that my parents had not come on to experience the wonderful view and the ride on the side of a hotel; it really was a terrific experience.

Knowing we had a long way back and having already gotten sore feet, we trekked back to the hotel. I was ready for bed by this time, even though it was only half past ten. My parents stayed at the bar eating multi-coloured nachos, and seeing as I couldn't be served for any alcohol I decided I would go up to the room with Hannah. It's no fun. What's the point in staying up when not only can you not drink but are given judging looks for looking young wherever you go. That's a curse I've had to bear for a while and probably will for years to come. So I decided against the idea even though my parents really wanted me to

stay with them. Instead, Hannah and I spent our first night in Vegas

watching Juno in the bedroom with a massive bag of potato chips.

Day Five – August 22nd

This morning we got to wake up in Las Vegas and experience our first full day here. Seeing as we are only here for two days, we have a lot to fit in. Today was the first day so far on the holiday that we had a lie in. I know 10am isn't a lie in to most people, but when you have spent the last few days getting up at 7am it's great. So today we didn't have breakfast, we went and had brunch. It was nice to just chill and get up when we were ready to without an alarm. The Sidewalk Cafe downstairs was our chosen place, where we had to queue to get in.

As we passed through the lobby, it shocked me that many of the people I had seen in front of fruit machines last night were still there. Old women with long grey hair all dressed in black and unusual sights of couples being brought drinks and change so they didn't need to move. The facial expressions and attire of some of the people made it clear they very rarely leave their seats, let alone venture outside. Each face looked withdrawn and transfixed by what they were doing that they hardly noticed anything around them. That's the beauty of a Vegas casino; they don't have windows or clocks - in order to keep the punters unaware of the time or weather. They would remain oblivious until it was made known to them. The look of exhaustion was written all over their faces, as they continued putting money in. It was a ritual they were unable to break; they didn't know when to stop spending or when the line of too much was crossed. They were surrounded by clouds of smoke and empty glasses, as they haven't banned smoking from public places in America yet.

After eventually getting into the cafe, we realised it was a buffet. It was decorated in dark wood and burgundy and had mirrors behind each of the tables. The floor was white and each waiter wore a waistcoat and a burgundy cumber band. Hannah and I went up first to report back with what was available, but as usual her plate remained pretty empty. She's very fussy with food she doesn't recognise. I am the same, as the mixture of bacon, eggs and potatoes contrasted with the fruit and giant pillar of cereals and yogurts was rather intimidating. I don't really like American bacon either, so that's one less thing I'll eat for a start.

"Is that all you are going to have?" My appetite is never at its best when we arrive anywhere new, no matter where in the world I am. For the first day, I always eat very little. In the Hard rock Cafe on our first night I had a starter of chicken wings and celery as my main mean, and now this morning I was picking at yogurt and fruit.

"I haven't decided yet."

Mum tutted and I grabbed and held down Hannah's leg to stop it bouncing. It's something I really can't stand. The table was moving and so was the long settee on our side of the table. As it stretched all down the one wall to cover the seating for all the tables, it's a wonder no one else felt it.

Pushing through the queues we each found something to have and settled down to eat, accompanied by the pulpiest glass of orange juice I have ever consumed. I hate pulp. So as much as I hated it, a fizzy drink with breakfast it was.

Today was about looking around some of the other hotels on the strip, the ones close by and ideally the more famous ones. We recognised the themes they each represented, and started off by exploring Caesar's Palace. This was the only hotel Hannah could identify, as it has appeared in films such as *The Hangover*.

"There's the desk from the film!" she shrieked excitedly running amongst the herds of people with her camera.

"Both of you pose for one" Mum directed us to a pillar away from the crowds for a picture, one which didn't have people constantly walking through it, practically impossible.

The inside had many similarities to our hotel with a casino to meet you as you came through the doors. Equally dark, the lobby had a large fountain with a statue of Caesar in its centre, with other Roman-like statues and wall art around it. The walls were decorated in water colours; the main lobby behind the reception desk was particularly colourful. There were large pillars dotted around, made of marble and designed perfectly for the era. Everything both inside and out was out of proportion and exaggerated, as if we were in a giant city living as ants. The ceiling was painted to look like the sky, pale blue with small clouds floating about. It looked so real that when you were walking the sky seemed to be moving with you and the clouds gave the illusion of gliding along.

The outside of the hotel had just as much detail as the inside. From giant gateways to a huge coliseum theatre around the side, the hotel's span was much bigger than I thought possible. The classic Roman archways and pillars continued on the sides and entrances to the building, along with the straight-edged, bold red font used on the title.

"Smile." The camera clicked again.

Just past the casino the hotel had its own mall. With shops such as Abercrombie and Fitch and Gucci lining the walkway, it is easy to see why many tourists have no desire to leave their hotels with so much to do. With another larger fountain situated in the middle of the shops, it felt like we were outside when we were just staring at the ceiling. Restaurants inside included The Cheesecake Factory, a well known American eatery famous for its exquisite cake making I now know, situated amongst the shops. We spent some time looking around and spent a fair amount of money on clothes and accessories. After spending a fair while in Caesar's, we decided to move outside and onto the next hotel.

"Another photo with all this in the background."

"I'm blinded, the sun's too strong. I can't see a thing."

Like that stopped her, Hannah and I were herded outside the coliseum and posed amongst the crowds.

After only a short walk outside, we were desperate to cool down again and ventured into the Mirage Hotel. This hotel has its own zoo, complete with an open dolphin pool, lions, tigers, alpacas and more. It was announced when we arrived that one of the tigers had given birth, but the cubs were not ready to be seen by people yet as they were only a few hours old. There was a display cabinet with tiger teddies and a billboard to signify the arrival of the cubs to the public which was a nice touch before the real ones were old enough to be seen. Instead, when we walked in we were greeted by lion cubs and a baby dolphin, which we were able to stroke whilst leaning over a low wall. A woman gave a demonstration about the dolphin when we entered, and swam through her legs and around the pool as she stood in the wet suit.

"What's he doing?"

We looked back after the initial entrance area to see Dad knelt down by the dolphin by himself, talking to it. There was no one around now and the pool was in the shade, and as we had turned back to see where Dad had gone, this is what we saw.

"Ian, come on."

"Yes yes," he waved us on, hinting that he would catch up. Very strange, must be the heat.

The whole area and footpath was shaded, so it was nice to be outside and also out of the heat. We were able to stop for a snack under a huge umbrella, whilst re-applying sun cream. Dad went to a cash point whilst my mum got us some drinks, and came back with a one hundred dollar bill. As it was the first one I have ever seen, I took a photo of it, before having the awkward moment of paying for a ten dollar purchase of celery sticks and coke with it.

"What are you doing with that? Don't put it on the floor." The ground was the one place I could get a clear shot of it without the light spoiling it. Hannah had her thumb on it, though we must have looked very strange. There wasn't any breeze, so where exactly was it going to 'blow?'

We didn't stay at the Mirage for too long as we had more to see, but we did go inside and rest at an ice cream parlour. The ice cream was soft and delicious, and cooled us down a treat. The sprinkles began to dye the ice cream, creating lots of rainbow lines before they sunk away from sight. Even indoors, the ice cream didn't survive. Here, there was also a mall and many casinos, but we decided to move on to the next place we wanted to see, having seen many shops and casinos already to last a lifetime. The ringing of the machines was quickly becoming insufferable.

"Let's go to that one next," Hannah pointed.

The last hotel we visited for now was the Venetian. As implied in its name, the Venetian is a replica of Venice and the whole hotel is like that of olden times in Italy. Outside on the street there was a pool filled with gondolas, which you could pay to have a ride on. The small boat would take you around the outside of the hotel and then continue inside and through the centre and the entire length of the building. The only catch was there were thousands of prying eyes looking down on you as you passed under them, looking like the obvious tourists riding a boat in a shallow pool. The pool was clear and rippled under the movement of the boats.

"Can we have a go?"

"No, you've been on the real thing. What would be the point?"

"It would be fun?"

"Look at it, it looks naff. Plus it's a rip off for what it is."

There was a reconstruction of St Mark's Square, filled with energetic masked dancers putting on a show in old Italian dress. The dancers were both men and women, and were mounted on a stage for all to see. They were dressed in distinct purples and greens with golden trim lining every crease. Almost like royalty or a ballet concert. The men wore tights, and each dancer had a beautiful handmade mask on a stick to complete their costume. There were also many quaint restaurants in the Square, with bridges going over the water and the beautiful sky painting on the ceiling yet again. It was so realistic, you felt like you had gone back in time.

"Pretty close to the real thing isn't it?"

I set off to explore the shops, leaving my family leaning over and watching the people on the gondolas. Each person was fake smiling as they came under the bridge and into the hotel, and saw the eyes watching them for the first time. I crossed a bridge and ended up doing a large loop around the water, passing many mask painting sessions and luxury soap shops along the way. This hotel didn't have the contemporary feel the former two did, and although stunning it didn't keep us occupied. There wasn't really a mall in this hotel; it was far too olden times for that. It had a few modern shops, but mostly it was a selection for specific tastes. All great to look at, but there's only so many soap shops, craft stalls and mask making classes you can look at. We stopped in one soap store and had a demo of some of the new products, they smelt great.

After the Venetian we stopped at a small supermarket for some bits, and whilst my mum went inside the rest of us gazed around at Treasure Island, another well known hotel with pirates decorating its exterior. Although we didn't venture inside or very close to it, we were intrigued by the detail the outside had. We had been in too many hotels today, and really didn't have the energy to see the same things in another one. The entrance had a giant pirate ship complete with model pirates to entice passers-by, whilst having the appeal of a luxury hotel at the same time. The walls were a smooth chocolate brown and there was pirate like decor of planks and ship wreckages all the way up to the door. Definitely keeping the theme alive. We jumped onto a moving walkway to take us back to our hotel, one with escalators and a conveyer belt motion combined. We went up and down on the walkway many times before our hotel came into sight, the lazy way to go from A to B that's for sure. But at least you didn't have the option of having to touch any hand rails. Halfway along was a group of wax models advertising Madam Tussaud's halfway between two of the escalators. It's a wonder they hadn't melted.

This evening we ventured over to the Paris hotel to have a look after a well earned break in the hotel room first. It was the one we had missed out deliberately as to come back to it when we could enjoy it fully. We decided to leave the full inside tour until tomorrow and just to embark on a trip up the Eiffel Tower, which stood life-size outside on the strip.

"An hour wait! Well we can forget that for tonight."

"Oh please, it won't be that long, they always say longer than it is."

"Hannah it's already late, we're all very tired. We will do it tomorrow."

"We could go and eat and then come back..."

"OK, we can try that."

One hour on and the wait time was still the same, even though there didn't seem to be any people about. We lurked amongst the slot machines briefly in the hope the time would change, and after asking we were assured the wait was still large.

"Sorry Hannah, we tried. We'll get here earlier tomorrow."

She pouted, and the ticket person looked at her and smiled. Who knows, the wait could be just as bad tomorrow, and if it was, we would have to just sit it out. All we knew was, we weren't leaving Vegas without going on it.

Hannah sulked all the way back to the hotel, no amount of jokes cheered her up. But it was an adventure that would still be there the following night.

Day Six – August 23rd

Today is the last day we will be spending in Las Vegas. In a way, it makes me sad to know that I may never get to come back here again, but I'm also excited to progress on our journey. Plus, if I ever do come back at least I'll be old enough to actually experience it! I know it's supposed to be flattering when you are mistaken for looking younger than you are, but there is only so much you can tolerate. I mean, there's being treated young, and being treated like a child.

It's still disturbingly hot, and has remained so for our entire visit, without even the slightest dip in temperature. We've had the type of heat where you feel more suffocated than contented, where it's not always comfortable to stay outside, and sometimes not even possible. Hannah and I decided that today we wanted to visit the Miracle Mile shopping centre, as we had passed it many times and were intrigued by what was inside. It was highly recommended by the hotel and many friends who have visited here in the past. Firstly though, it was breakfast time.

We headed down to the Paris hotel this morning and straight onto a French street. Well that's how it seemed. It even had signposts and paving, as well as the sky ceiling I mentioned earlier. We all ate in a sort of French diner, after what felt like a very long discussion about Hannah being too fussy to eat anywhere else. The inside was mostly counter based, and consisted of walking around the surfaces aimlessly with a tray until you found something you liked. It was clear that the place was popular, as when we arrived every seat was occupied and the only free table had the cushions from the seats missing, not that it stopped Hannah attempting to make herself comfortable on the bare panels.

"We can't sit on it like that," Dad persisted as Hannah tried to balance on the wooden frame. "Go and look outside the door."

The street area had a table free, and after it was cleared we managed to eat comfortably. A never-ending queue had formed opposite at another restaurant for an all-you-can-eat breakfast buffet. It was advertised a lot as a popular venue, but the line headed off into the distance. It was ridiculous. The poor waiter was rushing up and down the queue seeing how many people were in each party. Many starving customers gave up and went elsewhere shaking their heads and tutting. It then dawned on me that we were dining at the place where the hungry people came; the ones who didn't want to wait swarmed all the surrounding eateries in desperation. Hence why it was so difficult to get a table. I can't imagine the food would have been any better, and we had a much more attractive view of the synthetic blue sky and crowds of tourists. They would have just had four tie-dyed yellow walls and limited airspace, a frantic atmosphere that wouldn't be enjoyable to eat in. No matter how good the food was supposed to be. The walkway outside the diner was completely full of rushing bodies. There were groups of travellers constantly stopping to take photographs, striding business men with their suits and briefcases, and excitable children dashing off and being captured reluctantly moments later and hoisted into the air by their waists. Every doorway was filled with confused faces buried in maps, and the air was bursting with the clanging of cutlery and the sound of endless chatter. My parents had decided by now as we huddled around the breakfast table that they were going to explore the farther end of the strip, so Hannah and I ventured off to the mall for the afternoon.

Miracle Mile is a shopping centre situated about halfway down the Las Vegas strip. With big white lettering on a large red backdrop, it looked more like the entrance to Macy's than anything else. It even had the same style writing and layout. We entered the long and thin air-conditioned building and spent hours roaming shops that we had never even heard of. Anything to get out of the beating sun for a while, it was like being in a sauna 24/7. Hannah was immediately drawn to a souvenir shop, a safe option as we knew what to expect inside, well it's not like we haven't been in enough. It had banners swinging from the ceiling and just a few mingling tourists inside, analysing the items in great detail. They had everything from key-rings to shot glasses, clothes to bags, all branded "Las Vegas, Nevada" in jazzy fonts. You could even get personalised poker chips to take away. Each of these shops likes to put their own stamp on the merchandise, and some often have the same items at a lower price. That's why we were compelled to look in so many, though you need to be pretty patient for that. Hannah wandered round as if she had never been inside one in her life, wide eyed and pawing at everything, (We've spent more time in places like this than anything else, and we've only been here five days.)

After a few hours traipsing round, I was drawn to a stall selling giant beautifully patterned cloths that can be transformed into dresses. I'd seen many of these stalls dotted about but had never stopped to actually look at them. Intrigued, I approached the sales assistant who told me how "fashionable and easy to wear" they are. I could tell she wasn't going to let me leave without a sale. I really did want one, but they were very expensive. She was very persistent and made me feel I actually needed one in my life. So basically, I now own a large coloured piece of fabric that can be worn in "hundreds of ways." There was a TV screen with a model demonstrating how to wear this magnificent must-have. It's still just a piece of material at the end of the day, so $75 is a bargain? She saw me coming.

As we made the trek back to the hotel, bags in tow, Hannah starting moaning about being too hot. We had been inside all day so the heat hit us like a wall. We stopped for a rest on a nearby wall, panting. There was no cool place to stand, so we placed our bags down on the pavement in the best shaded area we could find. Suddenly, she let out a yelp.

"Look!" she was jabbing at my side and pointing to her arm. "That's from that bag!"

I stared at her arm and started laughing. "Oh my God! That's really funny."

The pattern from the souvenir shop bag had melted onto her skin, so the red, white and blue stripes were now inked onto her arm leaving not much left on the bag itself. It was sticky and stringy, like a she had fallen asleep on a newspaper. Though this was colourful and waxy.

"It won't come off;" she was persistently licking her fingers and rubbing at it, but it wouldn't budge. I just stood aside and giggled. "Well do something! It looks terrible."

The heat continued to scorch us as we stood still, so we went to a nearby soap and cosmetic shop that we had briefly visited earlier. It had sinks to wash off the soaps after you'd tested them, so I waited silently in the corner playing with some hand wash whilst Hannah scrubbed her skin and tried desperately to remove the American flag imprint from her arm.

After she was sufficiently satisfied the colour had faded, we carried on walking to the hotel. On the way, an old man on the corner of the street approached me.

"You like to dance eh? We go dancing?" He held my arm loosely in his fingers whilst swaying back and forth to symbolise dancing. "You look European, where are you from? Switzerland?"

When he eventually stopped asking questions for a moment I actually got to look at him, this silver haired old man who hung around plants on busy walkways in order to talk to young girls. His directness baffled me and I stepped back from him to get a better look. He wore casual clothes, and his face was covered by his beard. His facial hair was all the different shades of grey, and went right to the rims of his glasses. He had dirty nails and yellow teeth, and his breath was unbearable. I could barely understand his accent as it was, but he was staring straight at me waiting intently for his answer. I replied with the only way I could think of to get rid of him.

"I'm too young to drink in this country. And no, I'm British." I smiled in a sickly fashion.

He nodded in agreement and smirked.

"I'm from Bristol yes? England?" His arm was around my shoulders at this point so I shrugged him off and walked away, smiling and humouring him.

A blatant lie. For him to do that in the middle of a busy walkway when I have my thirteen-year-old sister at my side? Desperation springs to mind. Especially as he actually believed it was going to happen, like I was going to run off with him and go to some dance club in a country I don't even know? I tried to make out to Hannah that he hadn't bothered me, but the whole time I was stood there I was worried about what he might do. My parents weren't far behind us; I could see them in the distance leaving a shop, so the experience became slightly less scary. He was unfazed by my rejection, however, and just moved onto the next girl he laid eyes on.

After that ordeal was over with, we dumped our things in the room and headed for the pool whilst there was still some sunlight. We met our parents there as arranged, and after a rather impressive game of find the sunbed we set up for the afternoon. Hannah then decided this was her cue to vanish back up to the room again for a long time.

A long time passed and we were worried as to where she had got to. I was sent to find her and embarked on the embarrassing journey of going up 23 floors in the lift in my bikini to try and discover her. She was in the room; that much I could tell. There she was quite happily dancing about in my new 'dress'. Hannah is known for not taking very good care of possessions, so only on certain occasions is she allowed to borrow things. It's times like this when we have no choice but to spend time together that I remember how annoying she can be. It was an expensive item, one I shouldn't really have got. So there was no way she should be messing with it unattended. Fuming, I dragged her back to the pool and to this day she still isn't allowed to borrow that dress.

This evening, we decided to give the Eiffel tower another go. This time we managed it.

We queued for ages and were eventually stuffed into a lift crammed full of strangers, we were taken up by a woman with the boring job of being a lift operator. She must spend her days doing the two minute journey up and down the tower, I can't think of anything worse than my job requiring me to spend my days in a lift. Especially when the weather is continually so good outside. The smile on her face widened each time someone new entered the lift, and died as soon as the doors closed. When we got in, she was agitated. A "move back please" or a "and you sir" and a "you'll have to wait for the next one." Not one "it's beautifully clear up there tonight" or any happy/encouraging words to that effect. Instead, she tapped her foot all the way up; her gaze transfixed on the roof as she tried desperately not to make eye contact, she must have known down to the second how long the journey up took. I wonder how many times she does that trip in a day.

As we exited at the top, we were each greeted by the view of Las Vegas in all its glory. We could see the city from all angles, lit up with shades of every colour you could imagine. The sight that met us immediately reminded me of an air strip. The bulbs each perfectly placed, glowing symmetrically in their many colours. Each was a part of a giant puzzle; unless they all worked together the full image was not as spectacular. They each represented a hotel or event in the city, and were so bright you could see exactly where everything was placed. The buildings just blended into each other, like I imagine a forest would look if you decorated every single tree with fairy lights. Every inch of the strip shone, hundreds of thousands of lights, each important. They blazed back at me, nothing left untouched. I desperately fought with the mesh of the tower to take photos, the last thing I wanted was this view spoilt by black metal appearing in my pictures. Far to the right and left lay blank black canvas where the desert lay dark and motionless, segregated from the life of the party.

Although beautiful, the top of the tower was extremely stuffy, and with crowds of late night viewers queuing up desperate for a look our time was limited. The nights were no cooler than the days, and being shoulder to shoulder with people was very uncomfortable. The definite highlight had to be the bride and groom at the top taking their wedding snaps with the scene as a backdrop, her dress swished in front of her like a mermaid tail, everybody wanted to take their picture and make sure they were having a good time.

Having exhausted the tower and all around it, it was time to find somewhere to eat. We went to a restaurant my parents had previously visited in Florida, called Margaritaville. But as we are in Vegas, it was a lot more eccentric than we had anticipated. For a start, there was a volcano in the centre and the waiters weren't just regular waiters. It reminded me of the Hard Rock Cafe, if it was beach themed. The first waiter I saw was on the lower level, a pirate walking around on stilts and making balloon hats for everyone in sight. We were sat right by the volcano, which also doubled up as a bar. But just before our food came out, our waitress stripped off and began scaling the side of it. With the music blasting and everyone clapping, she danced along the top of the volcano, complete with lightning and rumbling sounds. She jumped onto a water slide hidden at the top, which took her through the fake rocks and to a large tank of green water right next to us, where she exited and bounced off to the beat of the applause. She was back moments later, dry and serving again.

I was so distracted by everything that was happening that I didn't even notice that my food was sitting right in front of me. I kept a wary eye on the waiters who were pulling people out of their seats and ramming hats onto heads involuntarily. I tucked into my food.

After the full rack of ribs defeated me, we all decided to go and watch the eruption of the Mirage hotel's volcano. Each night we had spotted from our hotel window people gathering to watch it, so as it was our last night we waded through the crowds to witness it for ourselves. The eruption was vast. The heat of the flames hit our faces from hundreds of yards away, even though we were leant on a fence shielded by bushes. The fire shot straight up in the air and changed colours as it bled down the side of the volcano, bursting in time to some dramatic music. At the foot, coloured water formed waves and jets appeared to shoot flames up into the air. Water and fire cascaded up into the sky and disappeared back into the pool of the volcano before beginning again. It was a show we had missed each night but was well worth finding and seeing. Despite the crowds and shoving, I'm glad we didn't miss it.

Now I am back in our room looking out at the activity below. There is never a quiet moment, places don't just close and people don't just go home, life continues all night and all day, every day. It's nice to sit in the cool and to actually rest at a comfortable temperature. After I've done my packing for tomorrow that is. We have an early start in the morning as we are leaving for San Francisco, so the alarm is set for 7.30. Another plane to catch and another place to visit. It has been a very tiring trip to date, but I have a feeling there is a lot more excitement to come.

Day Seven – August 24th

Today has been a very long day. After the very short flight we endured from LA to Las Vegas, the few hours up to San Francisco seemed to last ages. We got up early this morning to check out of the hotel, and I couldn't help feeling upset that we had to leave. I had a lump forming in my throat as we passed the motionless gamblers and waded through the sea of lights for the last time. It was so bright outside; I could see the speck of light pushing on the glass on the other side of the lobby.

Yet, it remained dark inside as the rituals were carried out. The walk over to the sunlight lasted a fair few minutes, and after glancing back for the last time the lights disappeared from my vision. But the sounds continued to overpower my ears, those persistent bleeps and jingles as the coins shot out will stay with me for a long time.

As we got out of the blazing sun and my burning nostrils had taken their final beating, our cab joined the long queue of cars trying to get away from the city. Every inch of tarmac was taken by vehicles and the view of brake lights that lay ahead seemed endless. For such a short journey, the winding traffic just wasn't moving and as lurking cars appeared from side streets the centipede of vehicles just seemed to extend with no sign of movement. The constant rage and horns blasting became so consistent that it was possible to drown them out and focus on other thoughts. I took my final looks at the over-exaggerated scenes we were leaving behind and the cascading buildings of a giant model village disappearing slowly behind us.

"Move your head." I was brought back to reality with an elbow to the face as Hannah practically clambered on top of me, desperate for a window view. "I'm trying to take a picture." You'd think that by now she'd have realised that the sheer glint of the glass was simply not going to allow this, but I kept quiet and allowed her to have her moment.

After arriving back at Las Vegas airport, the busy life seemed so far away as breezes of sand from the lonely desert roads brushed around our ankles. It was as though a five minute drive had taken us to another place, the hustle and bustle was gone and all that remained was one main road and distant plains of gritty sand. It was as if the city had been abandoned and signs of life stopped just two minutes from the strip. It was such a contrast: where were the masses of people? The excessive traffic we were stuck in? It was like the sand had swallowed vast amounts of civilization, like the life of the city only belonged in one place. Now the surrounding buildings were gone, it just made the sun beat harder onto my head, punishing us for venturing out onto exposed land.

The heat dimmed for the last time as we got inside, and I remembered why I liked this airport. Despite almost being sick the last time I was there, the surroundings just seemed to stick with me and I found I could quite happily have spent the day exploring what it had to offer. Ask me to describe the inside of Heathrow and I wouldn't know what to say, apart from the fact it has yellow notice boards. But this place managed to catch my eye in a weird way. For example, the seating in the departure lounge was lined up so we could see straight out onto the runway, no obstructions. The long strip littered with piles of sand lay in a pale shade of beige. The planes circling the tarmac were taking their time, before they were given clearance to approach. The row of windows in front of us allowed us to see everything, the sandy runway that made the sky look much brighter than it already was, perfectly clear as though someone had taken an eraser to it. The Internet actually worked too, and it was free. But I suppose with all the hotspots and gambling machines it was only natural that it would work. After all, if all those contraptions could use it why not a Blackberry?

The floor was a murky black, speckled with green like a swamp beneath our feet. The walls were a dingy white, dirtied from years of abuse from handrails and sticky fingers. The colour was sparse, like the entire inside had been drained of it and deposited right outside the window. The only colours were the blobs of impatient travellers and the lights projecting from the change machines and shopping facilities onto the walls and ceiling.

By now, it had got to midday and we had been due to board a while ago. Hannah was fiddling with her Ipod and sliding about restlessly whilst Dad messed about with the lock on his bag and Mum went off to get some snacks. Our flight had been delayed again, and after an extra half an hour of twitchy old men and fidgeting children we were finally able to board. We got on to a small red and blue plane and it was immediately obvious that we could sit anywhere. Hannah chose a seat for us further down on the left and our parents took some in the opposite row. The seats weren't particularly extravagant; in fact it felt more like I was on a bus than a plane. They were a greasy blue colour and glistened as though they were permanently wet. When you sat down you seemed to slide from side to side and my hair kept getting caught in the headrest. They clearly weren't made for people to actually sit in, all I had to do was shift slightly in order to get comfortable and I risked a spillage of yellow foam all over the aisle. The zip on my back pocket was grinding the leather the entire flight, and I knew my days were numbered before it broke through as it was wearing a hole beneath me; thank god it was only a short flight. They weren't comfortable and they certainly weren't sturdy. During take-off they rocked, so much so that I didn't even remember to look out of the window as we left the sand dunes and mountains. The heat was finally going, never thought I'd be glad to see the back of the sun for a while. The flight was pretty quiet, and the others that were on board were hidden behind the navy headrests which outnumbered all of us as we cruised through the Nevada skies.

After a few hours we landed rather smoothly back on Californian soil, a world away from the miles of copper landscape we had just crossed to get here. The temperature was certainly a change; I'd almost forgotten what wind felt like. The sky was charcoal and everybody was in a hurry to be somewhere away from you. The unfriendly welcome of everyone in sight barging around with their heads down became a problem when we realised we were miles from the hotel.

"Cab will cost you a fair bit, I think the train will be the best thing for you," said a large and podgy woman shielded behind some glass. She was clutching the microphone so tightly her knuckles had gone a different shade of pink and the dimples on her hands protruded outwards. "The machine is just over there." Her sausage fingers pointed the way to a ticket booth. As my parents followed her point, I couldn't help but notice her blouse straining as she moved; her elbow desperate to poke free from its tight prison. Her hair frizzed up from its intended position and she pushed it down with the palm of the pointing hand, making it clear she was done helping us.

We fussed for ages with that stupid ticket machine. Nothing about it made any sense, the buttons were just randomly placed and none of the options listed seemed to apply to us. And to make it worse, a large queue had formed and there was no one around to help, we dared not admit defeat to the scary booth lady. Our bickering was known to all the foot-tapping regulars waiting impatiently behind us, and just as the queue snaked around the corner our tickets finally began to print. We shuffled through the gate at that point and descended to the underground platform, looking at the ground to avoid any more attention.

The station looked like we were entering a theme park ride, as if we were going to shoot off out of the tunnel and onto something thrilling on the other side. That would have been a much better option, but instead we were stuck in a cramped carriage with crappy velvet seats and too many passengers, there were bikes in the gangway and people leaning on the doors. So we had to sit, for however long it was in a stuffy train with our suitcases rammed between our knees for a fair few stops before we could get off. I couldn't fault the scenery en route though; as we left the station the tunnel seemed to end high up in the air amongst all the buildings. We were the lone train that ventured through some of the city at the height of all interest. We twisted through the intimate spaces, right past windows and working people before dipping down to a lower level just as the sun was descending in the sky. Here, we joined some greenery and places out of the immediate public eye before the manic vibe of the real downtown life was upon us.

There was a schoolboy in our carriage, with his backpack on unaware of all that was going on around him. He remained plugged into his Ipod, subjecting all those around him to his taste in music. As he shuffled and bopped, I found myself wondering about his life, where he might live and what it must be like to go to school here. With that he got off, an ordinary boy going about his everyday life, completely unaware that his routine might be interesting to someone.

When we got off the train, the escalator leading up to the street stood still, so we had no choice but to drag our luggage up the steep incline, the wheels scraping every step. Or get a stranger to do it in Mum's case. We surfaced into the bustling heat of a San Francisco street right in the heart of the city. The sea was visible; San Francisco is so different from Las Vegas and much more industrial. Well that's what I've gathered so far whilst trying to keep up with Dad striding off into the distance. It was bright and breezy, and the sides of the roads were lined with clothes shops, offices and Starbucks. I was careful to watch my step at all times, the pavement drop to the road was deep, and Hannah regularly got her suitcase caught in the tram tracks. Just a few feet above us were dozens of cables, knotted together and perfectly positioned for the trams. All the buildings were back and away from the road, and blended together in one long line, as though none of them dared to extend a foot forward.

Knowing we were only two blocks from the hotel we strode on, especially knowing our friend Paul who had flown in from Florida to meet us was waiting. He'd flown in to spend Dad's birthday with us tomorrow, and now he was here waiting impatiently and we had no idea where the hotel was. We were the family walking gormlessly, holding up the pedestrian crossings and walkways. The ones who studied every street sign and dragged their luggage into everyone's way, so the sight of the hotel halfway down a side street came not a moment too soon. After eventually arriving at the Marriot it was a relief as we collapsed into comfortable burgundy sofas that embraced us in squishy leather.

About an hour after the kerfuffle had eased off, Paul told us about a bar he had discovered on the top floor called the "View Lounge" so we ventured up. Even the ride up in the lift intrigued me, as we had to swipe our key cards in order to get anywhere, so it didn't end well if you were caught in the lift without one as there was no way of telling which floor you might end up going to. The top of the hotel was a glass dome which enabled you to see right across the city and from many different angles. The sun had started to peek through the clouds and streaks of light were hitting some of the higher buildings. All the buildings from the window were beige coloured; and all seemed to merge together, almost fencing us in. Though thinking about it now, to someone else we were just another piece of that wall.

Over to the right we could see Alcatraz floating silently between gaps in the buildings. That is where we are going tomorrow for Dad's birthday, away from civilization.

After it got dark we took a bus down to Fisherman's Wharf (saving the tram for tomorrow) in order to get some food. We found a place on the pier called "The Player" which was completely sports themed. There were games, giant TV's playing the latest matches and all the waitresses were dressed as cheerleaders. There was a mini arcade scattered amongst the tables and all the walls and surfaces were plastered in scoreboards and basketball nets. The staff all wore black, and by the raging atmosphere it was clear that this was the place to be during major sporting events. We filled our starving stomachs, and caught up with each other's lives.

When we got back to the hotel, we got to our room we realised how small it was compared to the one in Vegas. Nevertheless, this view allowed us to look down onto the whole city and be amongst the entire goings on. We can see every light, hear every siren, but it's perfect. It's time to sleep now ready for the tour of Alcatraz and the birthday celebrations tomorrow.

Day Eight – August 25th

Today was Dad's birthday. We started this morning by having breakfast in Starbucks in the hotel lobby, so we could discuss plans and I could use the free internet for a while. Annoyingly, the internet only worked downstairs, and there was a large sum to pay for using it in the room. So I politely kept my emailing to the lobby. As it was only a small branch, the selection wasn't great. I'm not a big Starbucks lover, so nothing looked very appetising, and I ended up with a chocolate croissant of some sorts. The lumps of chocolate were strong and sickly, and a much darker shade of chocolate than I was used too. I pulled it apart for some time and finally forced it down; it just didn't taste right so early in the morning.

After Paul joined us, we took the long walk down to Fisherman's Wharf. He had booked last minute, and had to stay at the hotel across the road. This was unfortunate, but didn't make a lot of difference just for one night. It was very windy under the shadow of the buildings, but between each gap a streak of sun shot through and revealed a warm day and a cloudless sky. San Franciscans hate heat, according to the weather forecast, which said something along the lines of "Don't worry we'll soon be rid of this sun and be back to normal by the end of the week." Their weather is so predictable, never too hot and never too cold, which is what the citizens are used to. It is a complete contrast to the rest of California where the people thrive on being hot all the time, and for some it's a relief visiting San Francisco. Citizens enjoy the cool weather because it doesn't have the sticky humidity of other cities, and the temperature only varies about ten degrees most of the year. When the heat does come, it's only briefly, say about ten days a year, so everyone enjoys it when it arrives but looks forward to the original weather returning quickly. The fog varies according to which side of the city you live, as you get ocean spray on the one side and not the other, and with just two seasons, wet and dry, the temperature is almost always in the mid fifties.

On the walk down, Dad and Paul asked a policeman the quickest route to the pier so we were on time for our trip to Alcatraz. Mum, Hannah and I could hear them laughing and joking and pointing towards the sea before retreating back to us with the knowledge we needed to proceed.

The pier was a three mile walk, but because the weather was so pleasant it didn't seem to take us long at all. The five of us walked down through masses of giant buildings and streets lined with palm trees, and passed pillar box stands that displayed the day's news. Each building looked pretty much the same, all lightly coloured and each was taller than the eye could comprehend. It looks kind of how I expect New York to look, except with a hectic atmosphere. There was the added image of leaves cascading down the streets and swirling up around your face as you walked through the centre, with each building having them as a permanent fixture to their window frames. The pavements were spotless, and paved with large beige stones that always lay in the shade filled with hurrying people. It wasn't an overly busy atmosphere. We were passed the morning rush, so you didn't have people angrily pushing past you or being unfriendly, there was plenty of space for us to walk and stop to look at signs. There were lots of businessmen in long black coats carrying briefcases and speaking loudly on phones. Other business-types sat at their laptops in Starbucks, but there was no heavy traffic or masses of crowds anywhere.

A steep drop led us down from the pavement to the road as we dodged a tram to get to the other side. I did notice a significant amount of cracks in the road, where the tarmac had spilt in numerous earthquakes and been repaired several times. The most famous San Francisco earthquake happened in April 1906. It is remembered as one of the worst natural disasters in the USA and could be felt as far away as Oregon. The death toll was estimated at around three thousand people, the biggest loss of life in a natural disaster in California's history. Ironically enough, many prisoners from various San Francisco jails were housed at Alcatraz after the earthquake's devastation. As I snapped the sights I was surrounded by, it dawned on me that we were in a place where an earthquake could come at any time. I shook that idea off briskly, knowing it would bother me all day if I didn't.

Our trip was due to leave at 12.30, so we had to be there and in the queue in plenty of time. Paul led us down an endless line of piers, which stretched way off into the distance. Big wooden structures stuck out all along the sea front, each jammed full with shops and restaurants, and the Port of San Francisco. In some cases, you weren't even aware you were on a pier until you passed through all that was on offer. Each Pier had its number flying on a flag at its entrance, and looked straight out at Alcatraz and the scene of boats in the mist. The long line finally led us to Pier 33, where the queue was no better. There was a large food stall where the pavement met the pier and also a restaurant and small gift shop. All the buildings looked like derelict warehouses, battered by the sea air on the outside but transformed for tourists to shop and eateries on the inside. The concessions were overpriced, and Hannah reluctantly settled for a bottle of water before elbowing her way back through the crowds to join us. The system was very strict; there were no purchasing tickets on the spot or trying for an earlier ferry as you were flatly refused. Each trip was full and the line soon snaked round through three rows of rope barriers.

The area was bustling, and a small marquis sheltered us from the sun as we prepared for boarding. Before we were allowed onto the ferry, each party had to stand in front of a backdrop of Alcatraz and pose ridiculously, so not only could everyone queuing behind bask in your stupidity, but the pictures were then displayed for the other trips of the day to view as they lined up.

The ferry over to the island lasted twelve minutes. To avoid the lazy tourists we sat up on the roof to get the most of the experience. We were very exposed, but the front of the boat started off by shielding us from the wind. But the further from the city we got, the more violent the wind became, whipping my hair into my face and making me shiver profusely. The entire top deck was white. White benches, white flooring, and white railings keeping us back from the sea below. Even though it was clear and sunny I was so glad I brought my hoodie. The city slowly got further away and was highlighted under a spotlight of sun; the colour remained behind as we headed through the grey sea with a hovering grey mass above us. The Golden Gate Bridge was in the distance at this point, masked by a heavy layer of mist, the top of it completely gone. It was a deep red, almost burgundy, standing out through the sheet of fog with the grey water nipping at its ankles. The fog grew thicker as it reached the sky, so I was unsure how much of the bridge I couldn't actually see. To my left, Alcatraz was floating closer and closer.

After docking next to a giant concrete pier, we were instructed to head towards a man on a podium waving his arms. Everybody immediately flocked towards him, but Hannah headed off to a stand selling a leaflet about the island. The leaflets were there for the taking, and you were just supposed to put your money down a chute.

"How would they know if we just took one?" said Hannah, peering over her shoulder as she spoke.

"I don't know. I bet they would though. It's only a couple of cents so just put it in the tube."

"I wasn't going to *actually* do it, I was just saying." She threw her change into the slot and sauntered off, leaflet in hand.

After a brief introduction, the man on the podium shooed us off and left us to fend for ourselves. We followed the swarms of tourists up two steep inclines, taking in the views as we climbed. People in golf buggy-like vehicles kept shooting past, ushering people out of the way. This was the lazy way up the hill, for those who couldn't, and those who couldn't be arsed.

"I want to go in one of those," Hannah bleated, "I'm sick of walking."

I ignored her whining as I could see the main prison building up ahead, and Mum, Dad and Paul were already queuing to get inside. We had to queue to receive our headphones and cassette for our guided tour, the line led us through a room where lockers, prison uniforms and showers were. The uniforms were folded and placed on top of each locker, whilst some were hanging on a clothes horse, waiting to be collected and worn as they had been all those years ago.

The tour began, and everyone split up and pressed play on their cassettes as we entered the main prison. The rooms were filled with hundreds of gormless tourists walking around with their heads in the air and their mouths wide open, stroking every possible surface and grabbing the bars of every cell. It was silent – everyone was so transfixed by what they were hearing, no sound could be heard; it was eerie but suited the atmosphere perfectly. The voice of a correctional officer guided you down each row of cells, sending you to different ones and explaining what happened inside it. From time to time a prisoner's voice would come on, saying who he was and that I was standing in his cell. I heard "I am Roy Gardner, inmate AZ-110, and this is my cell." He told me about the possessions I could see and why he had them, the sound of voices behind him indicating prison surroundings. There was a poster on one of the walls. It read: "Break the rules and you go to prison, break the prison rules and you go to Alcatraz." This of course and the others surrounding it were there purely for the tourists, though the information they provided was invaluable. Like actually being able to see someone's face as they spoke to you made you feel the experience even more intensely. It is a well known fact that Alcatraz was never used to its full capacity, only ever having 302 of a possible 366 inmates.

One of the main prison rules was: "You are entitled to food, clothing, shelter, and medical attention. Anything else you get is a privilege." Number 5, Alcatraz Prison Rules and Regulations, 1934. It was a place of high risk where only the uncontrollable were sent. No female correctional officers were allowed and no female prisoners were ever sent there. Despite its reputation and strict rules, like being up before 7am each day, no executions ever happened on the island.

Each cell was a carbon copy of all the others, each containing a bed, a sink, some shelving and a bedside table. What surprised me was that all the cells had pink bars, making it seem less scary. The inside was also decorated half pink and half green, giving it a brighter look. Al Capone's cell was B-181, residing on the second floor. As you stood at the end of each row, it was like looking at a sandwich: brown floor, two tiers of salmon-coloured bars and a brown ceiling. Each strip of cells was named after a famous area, for example Broadway, Park Avenue and Times Square. The inside of the building was generally light, with skylights and lots of windows. The tape guided me into a few cells and told me to close the door, to give me an idea how confined the inmates actually were. It was different having a one-on-one tour, being able to stop and rewind wherever necessary, but every so often I caught sight of a bewildered Hannah where she had clearly lost her place and was trying desperately to catch up.

"I don't know where to go. Help me" I'd get every so often.

"Look, I can't help you, just stop messing with the tape and carry on."

Each cell had a window nearby, and the second floor was able to look straight out at San Francisco which lay so close by. It was designed this way so they were reminded every day exactly what they were missing.

Every once in a while I caught sight of one of my party, but they were so engrossed I never got their attention, just the odd smile. The tape directed me to some pictures on the wall, like one of the famous inmates who had served a sentence. Each image had their name, their reason for being there, where they were transferred from and how long they were at Alcatraz. Alphonse "Scarface" Capone the notorious American gangster was transferred from Atlanta and served time for tax evasion for five years at Alcatraz. Capone was publicly criticized for his supposed involvement in the Saint Valentine's Day Massacre, when seven rival gang members were executed. He was also known for smuggling illegal alcoholic beverages into the city and also engaged in the bribery of government figures and prostitution. After arriving in Alcatraz, he was stabbed by an inmate with a pair of shears in the queue for a haircut, and Capone's sentence was doomed from then on.

Robert "The Birdman" Stroud was transferred from Leavenworth prison to Alcatraz in 1942 and remained there until 1959. He was serving a sentence for murder and despite his nickname; he actually only kept birds at Leavenworth penitentiary, prior to being transferred to Alcatraz, where he was not allowed to keep pets. Stroud's love of birds was later made into a film, "The Birdman of Alcatraz" which portrayed a fictional version of his life. Out of boredom, Stroud adopts a sparrow as a pet. Before long, he built up a collection of birds and cages, and when they fell ill, he made experiments and came up with cures. As the years pass, Stroud becomes an expert on bird diseases and even publishes a book on the subject. The film is still very famous, and on television a lot. It stars Burt Lancaster as the lead role it was nominated for best actor in a leading role in 1962.

Behind the rows of cells was a corridor which had a ladder up to the roof for emergencies. The corridor was always locked, so it was unlikely someone would search there for a missing prisoner. A guard was stabbed with a spoon in one incident when some inmates attempted to get his keys late at night. Another man called Allen Clayton West made a

95

fake head and put it in his bed as part of his escape plan. I was directed to the cell where the fake head lay in the same position as it was at the time, duvet up and leaving just the hair and some skin on display. This attempt was part of the mass breakout plan in 1962. Unfortunately, despite his efforts, West never made it out of his cell on time, leaving brothers John and Clarence Anglin and Frank Morris to escape without him.

John and Clarence Anglin and fellow inmate Frank Morris were successful in their escape as they attempted to swim from the island to the San Francisco mainland. A distance of 1.5 miles in treacherous currents and freezing conditions. Each inmate dug a hole in the wall of his cell using an instrument they had acquired from a broken vacuum cleaner and some barber tools, hiding their plan behind an air vent before eventually reaching the other side. After long months of preparing, the men had gathered all the gear they needed for their escape. John Anglin carefully completed the valve assembly on a large six-by-fourteen-foot raft, while Morris modified an accordion-like instrument called a concertina, which would be used to rapidly inflate the raft. But while they had achieved their goals, West had fallen behind in digging out the vent at the rear of his cell. His job had been to construct special wooden paddles for the raft, so he didn't need to leave his cell. On the night of June 11, 1962, Morris announced that the top vent was loose enough, and that he felt that they were ready to attempt the escape. As West had fallen behind, the others had no choice but to leave him, and were last seen heading towards the cell house roof that night. This is the most famous escape as they actually made it down to the water. Their plan was very complicated, as their water rafts and life preservers were made from over fifty rain coats that came from other inmates some donated and some stolen. It is still unknown to this day if they made it, as the strong current and freezing water is likely to have killed them if nothing else.

The tape told stories and incidents of the prison for a full two hours, leading me to the control room, a manikin in guard's uniform and to the kitchen. I found the kitchen and dining area very intriguing. I was able to listen to the sounds of food fights and cutlery banging, as well as men fighting and being pulled apart. Dinner time was the most dangerous part of the day, as many deaths occurred at meal times. The voice lured me over to the kitchen and allowed me to see how sealed off it was from the cafeteria. Where the large knives hung, a large silhouette of the implement was painted behind each one, this was so if any went missing staff were immediately aware of what utensil had gone and the danger they were dealing with.

The last stop on the tour was outside, to a beautiful courtyard that overlooked the sea and the city. There was a large building which was home to the prison guards. No women were prisoners, so relatives of the guards were the only females to ever be on the island. Like the windows, the yard was deliberately overlooking the bay, forcing them to look at civilization and the world going by without them. The tape ended, and we were escorted through the gift shop to wait outside. Mum, Paul and I finished on time.

"Did you enjoy that?" Mum was on me the second I was outside. "Wasn't it interesting?"

"I enjoyed it more than I thought." My eyes were drawn to an impatient Paul tapping his hands on a railing as it was clear he was ready to leave. "Where's Hannah?" I asked.

"She got confused, meddling with the buttons on the cassette and ended up being lost. Think she found her way eventually, hopefully she's nearly done."

Paul began pacing the walkway, tapping his pockets and fiddling with his phone. He never was one to keep still. "He's got ants in his pants" Mum would always say, as he never liked to be anywhere for too long. I never knew how he and Dad had gotten along so well, as Dad will drag out any process and act like nothing has a time limit. With Paul, you need to have pinpoint co-ordinated plan for each day, you have to be on this bus by this time, eaten by this time, washed and changed by this time you get the idea. He's always early to everything, whereas we are always late. He tuts when he thinks we aren't looking and starts walking off in the direction of the next destination as a hint that everyone else will follow. Sometimes he's good to have around, when you want to fit everything in. Other times, he's a pain.

I didn't need to ask about Dad, he's known for going off on tangents. He was wandering off to places like the sports yard which weren't included on the tour. He found the history fascinating and decided that going round a few extra places wouldn't hurt. I spotted him a few times and had wondered why he was so far behind me, but he was spending a long time studying each item. He was ages, so when Hannah finally appeared moody and irritable I went back to the gift shop to look at some books written by some of the inmates.

It was still bright and breezy when we left the island on the 3.15pm ferry, back on the top deck. It was clear everybody was cold by the look on their scrunched up faces. The wind was still aggressive and the water was a little choppier, and Hannah's whining started up again.

We decided to get a snack on Pier 39 when we got back. Pier 39 is where we were briefly last night, and is famously known for being home to a lot of sea lions. They can clearly be seen basking on a jetty in their many groups, and have recently acquired their own billboard: "Happy 20th anniversary sea lions of Pier 39."

"Aww look at them," Hannah cooed, pulling out her camera, "look, look how they're all on top of each other."

"I'm surprised that jetty can hold them," said Mum, "they're massive."

Dad and Paul wandered off and were seen leaning over a wall further down, pointing out at where we had just been.

Other tourists began pointing at the sea lions, most with the same theory. Each picked up their children to look at the "big seals," and elbowed their way to the patch of wall with the best view.

Their dark brown skin shone as they lounged and jumped in and out of the water. They howl all through the day and night, and can be heard on surrounding piers hundreds of yards away. They are a main attraction of San Francisco, and even have signs advertising them: "Follow Salty the sea lion to see the California sea lions."

Paul chose a place for a snack on the pier called "Wipeout." whose slogan was "The only good suit is a wet suit." We sat outside as the sun began to dim and shared a large platter of chicken, fish, salad, chips and onion rings.

"Are you sure that'll be enough for all of you?" said the kitted up waiter anxiously, even though the plate could easily have fed another mouth. Mum looked up at him in disbelief, chicken in hand.

"Oh God yes, more than enough." She rolled her eyes. How could all this not be enough?

This later led to looking in a few of the shops. My favourite was called "Lefty's, San Francisco – The Left-handed Store." It had everything from left-handed pens to notepads that started at the back, even watches where the numbers went around the other way. It was truly backwards but I loved it.

On the way back to the hotel, after a lot of sulking, Hannah was allowed to ride on the outside of the tram. We jumped on at Fisherman's Wharf as it began to get dark; obviously the time everybody else needed a tram too. It wasn't at all safe as we were literally bursting out of the sides, and it was packed and with people diving on and off at every junction, the jostling was continuous. The journey was bumpy that as I hung onto the bar I could still quite as easily have fallen out. The hills were so steep that it felt as though the tram was vertical some of the time, switching between facing straight down and straight up rather frequently. The ride took us on the path of a wave, rippling up and down and ascending more than I thought possible. How could we possibly get any higher? The roads were so unpredictable that I began to feel quite queasy and with the driver yelling "hold on!" at sharp junctions the thudding stops certainly weren't helping. The brakes on the tram were very good I have to say. We stopped quickly every time, though never comfortably. After banging my head a number of times on the pole I was able to give my poor aching hands a rest and let go. I spent the last few stops when it was quieter sat on a bench slightly further in from where I was stood. Although it was just a slab of varnished wood I was glad to stretch out my fingers and massage my palms.

A freshen up and a drink in the "View Lounge" later and we were off to Macy's and the "Cheesecake Factory." Macy's was all shut up late in the evening, and after trying many entrances to get in it began to get tedious. A few laps of the block later and we made it inside. Famous for its cheesecake, the restaurant was packed; even waiting for a table became a problem as we were continually in the way. It was dimly lit, with the main source of light coming from the cheesecake counter. We had a booth tucked away in the corner and the lack of personal space was beginning to make me feel quite sick. I failed to finish my massive portion of pasta and skipped having a cake altogether, just picking at Hannah's from time to time to show I was making the effort.

Walking back was horrible, I felt really sick and it was cold, so at gone midnight I was glad to welcome my bed. Now I'm all settled and feeling better I can look forward to our last full day here tomorrow when we tackle the Golden Gate Bridge. It'll be great to see it properly up close, not just a view from a distance on a ferry. We will be riding over it on bikes first thing in the morning, though Paul has left today. I'm getting the feeling he didn't want to ride the bridge...

Day Nine – August 26th

Today was our last day in San Francisco. I'm sad because this is the place I've enjoyed visiting the most since we've been away. Granted, the weather isn't really ideal as I prefer being hot, but the general vibe of the city has made me love it. Plus, it has been a welcome change after being in Vegas the past few days. I have loved all the activities we have done since we came here, even though today has been utterly miserable. Although no rain actually fell, the sky was smeared with grey all day, like when you blend a pencil drawing to remove all the lines. All the clouds merged into one like the British weather we had left at home just over a week ago. It was windy, cold, and damp and out to sea it was very foggy.

We began this morning by having breakfast in Starbucks. Not the one in the lobby, one a bit further away en route to Fishermans Wharf. It was quiet, considering where it was placed. And, it had a lot more variety in what it sold. Hannah and I took a seat by the window whilst

Dad ordered and Mum faffed about getting the key to the toilet. I was tired; my head was resting on my fists as I sat looking out of the window and daydreaming. I was staring so intently at the random people walking past that a poke to the side came as a bit of a shock.

"Look! Look at that woman, what is she doing?" Hannah doesn't do discreet.

I looked up. Outside the window was an old Chinese woman rooting through the bin. She had opened the little door on the side and had the inner can stood on the pavement, she was peering right to the bottom and lifting things up into the light. She was armed with a black bag and was pocketing anything interesting or edible. Dad was sat with us by this time. We all sat looking at her as she grovelled deeper.

"She's really set on rummaging in there," said Dad. "Maybe she's looking for something in particular."

She dug away, this small grey-haired woman in what looked like a nightie, filling her bag with rubbish. No one walking past took any notice of the strange vision; I guessed she must be a regular.

A little while passed and the woman pulled something out from the bottom of the bin. It was inside a grubby carrier bag. It didn't look like much, but the look on her face was triumphant. She pulled out the item and held it in the air.

"Is that?" Dad paused.

"Oh my God it is."

The woman stood in front of us admiring a pair of battered old trainers. Old and worn, yet you'd think they were brand new with the smile on her face. She must have hidden them there, why else would you go looking for them? She threw off her flimsy shoes and put them on before returning the bin to its original position. With that she was gone.

"She put them there," said Dad, "or she watched someone throw them away and went back for them. If not her then someone else would have had them." He laughed and started to nudge me. "Different way to stay the day wasn't it? Eh?"

Neither Hannah nor I answered. We sat messing with our drinks and food until it was time to leave, mulling over the sight we had just seen.

After breakfast, we made the long trek down to Fisherman's Wharf. To get there from where we were, we had to go through Chinatown. Chinatown was so surreal, with just an underpass separating it from the main city it is now a recognised town and culture in its own right. The closer we got to the Wharf the more it trailed away, but the time we were there made us feel like we were in an oriental country and reminded us of Hong Kong. Although it only spread a short distance, it went back quite significantly hiding many buildings behind the main street. Many festivals such as the International Dragon Boat festival, the Chinese Culture Center Spring festivals, as well as events like the New Year Basketball Jamboree and the Chinese New Year Flower Fair are held throughout the year. Known as the largest Chinatown outside Asia, it was hard to believe we were actually in America. It has been home to Chinese immigrants since 1848 and has been developing rapidly ever since. It became more determined than ever to excel after the fire from the earthquake of 1906 destroyed most of its earlier structures. It now has a bank, a library, many schools and churches and even a YMCA. The main road was lined with stalls and shops with little flats above them. The stalls were cramped and sold many things from fruit and vegetables to fish, all of which were still writhing on the ice counters. There were baskets surrounding the stalls filled with nuts and dried fruit all priced in Chinese. Every road sign was Chinese and there weren't really any Americans around at all. The 1920s saw more buildings become decorated with pagoda-like roofs and the lampposts were decorated with dragon motifs, and colour was finally brought into the town. It was impossible to walk in a straight line, as to avoid the constant flow of people and wicker baskets you had to continuously swerve. A different culture had built its life in the midst of San Francisco, one which was bustling and happy, it even has its own beauty pageant of *Miss Chinatown* and has its own newspaper. The sights of colour and culture bring plenty of visitors every year; and in fact it is more popular than the Golden Gate Bridge for tourists. Although we were only passing through and didn't experience any of the restaurants, I really enjoyed visiting it.

We knew we had reached the end of Chinatown as the hills and traffic started to appear again. The hills were excessively steep, so much so that the other side went up higher than my eye-line. Each one is like a V shape, with the kink in the middle where two hills meet. We were stood at the top of one side and were what seemed like miles from the bottom. Each of the sides was fully packed with cars as this area was residential. The roads were bumpy and cracked and didn't have any markings on them. They looked as if they had been jigsawed to the adjoining roads in all the wrong places.

"Bet they have strong handbrakes," Dad joked at the cars parked millimetres from the bumper in front. I wouldn't be so keen to park there I'll tell you that much.

It was ridiculous how steep they were. It would be an absolute killer to walk it, and as for snow I wouldn't even like to think about it. I just felt sorry for the people who lived on them but also how fit they must be. I bet they don't even consider it steep anymore, not that we saw anybody walking up it at that time.

Dad stood still staring in all directions. He was still standing there when we were ready to leave. We were in a city that has over fifty hills that looked like this one, considered one of the hilliest places in the world, and he was stood still.

"This is where they filmed *Bullitt*."

I nodded and smiled to humour him. He clearly liked the film and was glad to be in the place where it was shot. Though none of the rest of us had seen it, or could relate to it, we remained bored just staring at a piece of road for over ten minutes.

We reached Fisherman's Wharf not long after that and went to the kiosk of "Blazing Saddles" (Yes, another film reference) bike rental. We were handed a map of the many routes we could take as well as being measured for our bikes and helmets.

"Your trousers are a bit long," the guy was pointing at my linens. I was told to dress in longer trousers so I didn't keep catching my ankles on the pedals, and he goes and says this. "You'll have to tie rubber bands around them."

I ignored the sniggers from my family as he returned with white elastic bands to go over my black linens. He couldn't just put them round once though, oh no. He looped the bands three times around my ankle to stop my linens blowing and getting caught on anything. They were far from fetching with my daps. Needless to say it looked totally stupid. The guy looked pleased with his work and went off in search of some large helmets.

"Do I have to wear one of these?" Seeing how stupid Hannah looked in hers I really didn't fancy wearing it. Plus, it was so uncomfortable and its lining was sticking to my hair. Never did like the fact they put Velcro inside them.

"Owh," his tone was patronising. "Sorry, only over eighteens get the choice not to wear one."

Another massive snigger from my family in the background, turning their heads as if I hadn't noticed.

"Well I'm nineteen and I don't want to wear one." I looked at him and smiled. I hoped I'd made him feel stupid, (hopefully as stupid as I felt with rubber bands around my legs.) I stood my ground and wouldn't wear one, just to prove my point. Then after analysing the route we would be taking I decided to change my mind. I didn't want to be veering off down hills at high speed to fall off and have a lecture about it later on. My whole family had one on, so I reluctantly decided it was for the best.

Dad decided he would be the one to navigate. Though this literally meant following the people in front of us. He pedalled off ahead and was annoyed to find us all lagging behind. It was a main road and I was getting my bearings on an unfamiliar bike on the wrong side of the road, so I wasn't going to be fast straight away.

"Where are your mum and sister now?" he asked when I caught up. They could be seen lagging behind when it came to riding uphill. I kept forgetting about being the wrong side of the road, and ended up swerving a number of times. When there were no cars it's easy to fall into habit and go off to the other side once in a while, but when the traffic does come it isn't fun for anybody.

It was utterly freezing. The wind was blowing into our faces as we rode, beating at our skin like tiny fists. My cheeks were raw, my hands were dry and it was much easier to keep going than to stop. I finally got up to Dad's pace but the other two were still far behind. Within the first fifteen minutes of the two and a half hour ride Hannah had knocked her chain off. I found this impossible to understand as she wasn't spending that much time actually *on* the bike. People were gliding past as we had entered a park area, where we had to administer to Hannah's damage. The sky was black at this time and we feared for rain at any time. On a bench, Dad flipped the bike.

"Only you could do this," he scowled at Hannah. "We've barely started yet."

"It's not me! There's something wrong with it!"

His hands were covered in oil but he managed to fix the problem. Hannah tried defending herself but it's in her nature to break stuff. Thank God for my packet of wet wipes or else he'd have been filthy all day.

After that we were off again. It wasn't long before Mum and Hannah were pushing their bikes and falling behind which slowed us down a lot. We couldn't afford to be separated when so many other people were doing the same course. We stopped at a rest stop a bit further along as it was indicated on the map. It was an abandoned warehouse on the banks of the river which had been converted to a souvenir shop/cafe.

The warehouse overlooked the Golden Gate Bridge, and was very close to it. At least at that point we knew there couldn't be much farther to go.

"It's so cold. I'm freezing..." I looked pleadingly at Dad who had a jumper around his waist which he wasn't using. He handed it over and we sat down on a bench outside with our bikes. Hannah still wasn't happy and threw her bike to the ground.

"Something's wrong with it. It's broken," she whined.

"No, it's just you."

"You try it then."

Determined to prove her wrong, I grabbed the bike and rode around in a circle. I looked completely stupid with my knees up by my elbows as it was clearly too small for me.

"It's fine, see. You're jus..." as I went to get off, the bike slid on the gravel beneath me and I fell straight off sideways.

Hannah was hysterically laughing. I didn't bother with trying to justify what had happened. Everyone still saw and it was still funny.

There was a hill around the back of the warehouse that exaggeratedly zigzagged upwards until it got to the Golden Gate Bridge. The further up we got the mistier it became. All we could see was sky and water, and the brake lights of cars crossing the bridge. Even the bright scarlet framework was disguised, its head and shoulders masked in the fog. This meant it was impossible to tell how tall it really was; even when we were directly under the highest point we couldn't see anything. Which was disappointing, I'd so hoped I'd be able to enjoy it properly. In reality, I had no better view of it now than I'd had on the ferry to Alcatraz. We rode along the jam-packed pavement as the cars whizzed along beside us and disappeared into the fog. It was like being inside a snow globe, surrounded by thick cloud and mist the further in we got. We stopped halfway where the pavement extended for us to do so in order to soak up the experience. The bridge was bitterly cold and I couldn't stay still for long. With so many people trying to do the same thing, trying to stop and dismount a bike was increasingly difficult. We were separated a few times and had to keep stopping and waiting as the rest of us weaved to get closer. The mist was descending more and more as we came to exit the bridge and it became unbelievably dark.

We left the bridge and made it to a look-out point where we could look back on what we had just achieved. The bridge had a grey haze looming around it and the people cycling it were barely visible. We took the time to try and see out where we had come from but it was too foggy. All I know is that we seemed to be riding it for a long time. Dad got the map out and pointed in the direction we needed to go next.

Before I knew it we were flying down a dusty road with sharp bends and speeding cars. It was quite dangerous really. There was nothing to stop us riding straight over the edge and down into a ravine. Being so high up the drop was huge, so for a bike trail for all ages it wasn't very safe.

"Julia! Wait" I could hear Mum calling as her and Hannah had slowed right down. They didn't like this bit at all and were being over-taken all the time. Dad on the other hand was flying down, feet off the pedals leaving clouds of dust behind him. I wanted to go fast so shouted back for them to hurry up. I wasn't going all that fast yet anyway, I hadn't built up enough momentum. If a car came up and frightened me I'd be straight over the side so I was lagging behind a bit myself. Some of the other people doing the trail were clearly professionals. It was obvious not only by what they wore but the tutting that came when you got in their way and stopped then from speeding off.

The further down the hill we got and the brighter the sun became, the clouds lifted as we headed into little Sausalito. It was small and didn't have a lot to offer as a town, but what it did have it spread out as much as possible. It had rows upon rows of hilltop picture-book houses with verandas and picket fences. The walls were all brightly coloured and no two looked alike. They crept down to the main road which consisted of no cars and a few random eateries. There was an area to leave your bikes as you came down the steep hill and came amongst the residential surroundings. One bike park for all these people, all of which had exactly the same bike as you and the same helmets. This would be fun later. You had the option to hop back on the ferry or to stay and explore a while. There was no way I was taking the third option of cycling back, not a chance. We had been following a map and cycling for nearly three hours so we wandered down the road away from the crowds to get a snack. It was a way to get people to visit the town, but there wasn't enough there to stay indefinitely.

We found a strip of restaurants alongside the water and a small dock. It was ghostly, houses and roads but the further we walked the fewer signs of life we saw. We ate in a place called "Paradise Bay" which was very peaceful without many customers. Plus, it was the only place that had something Hannah would eat. We each had something small, (as it was very pricey) and compared the sunburns on our faces and heads. I was amazed by the sunburnt streak I had down my nose considering the weather had been so miserable, but we had all caught it from cycling in the wind we guessed. We sat on a wooden deck with large parasols and looked at the boats sitting in the mud. There were people tending to their sails and sitting on the jetty as the sun began getting dimmer. We sat and watched them for a while before getting the motivation to get the ferry back over to gloomy San Francisco.

Just before six, we got the ferry back to the pier. The ferry was huge, much larger than the one to Alcatraz. But it did have to accommodate everyone as well as their bikes. So imagine, hundreds of people are on board this ferry with you and they've all got bikes from the same rental place? Even if you manage to find yours in the bike park, getting them onto a ferry with twice as many people means it's pretty much impossible to find the ones you came with. Mum decided on a way for us to make sure we had the right ones. Each bike had a pouch on the front, to which she attached a small branch. So we were the family with a branch stuck to our bikes rather than just tying a jacket to the handlebars. The steward loved the idea however, and applauded Mums individuality.

The contrast from where we had been to where we were going was significant. We seemed to pass through a barrier of light and enter into the mass of grey on the other side. On the hills of Sausalito there was a massive shadow as the houses remained in the sunlight and the scenery gradually faded into darkness. The riverbanks became grey and the water was choppier, even some rain started to speckle as we travelled across the water.

After returning our bikes to the kiosk we ate tea in the "Bubba Gump" restaurant on Pier 39. The restaurant overlooked the water and the journey on which we had just embarked. The restaurant itself had a vintage feel and was full of happy families.

"Two children's menus?"

"No. I mean no thank you. Just the one." I took the menus from the waitress and slid into our booth. Bubba Gump is a Forest Gump restaurant with pictures and quotes from the film plastering the walls and tables. Hannah asked for lemonade, and was answered with:

"Which flavour? We have blueberry, raspberry..."

"Blueberry please."

Well, I have never seen such a vile drink in my life. Out came a tall glass of pale purple liquid with giant blueberries floating at its surface. It was lumpy and very sour, and none of us liked it at all. The blueberries were blocking the straw which made it impossible to drink. It was like a chemical reaction in a plastic cup. Though we did finish it between us to get our money's worth, Hannah sure as hell wasn't going to drink it.

We had a flip board on our table. One side read "run Forrest run!" and the other "stop Forrest stop!" It was a really quirky and popular place, with various shots of Tom Hanks brightening up the walls. It keeps the fame of the film alive and is a real success to the locals and tourists.

There was a really fat man on the table next to us with the biggest meal I have ever seen. He had so many plates surrounding him heaped in fries and chicken bones and had a napkin tucked into his t-shirt. The button on his jeans bulged as his stomach flopped over the top of them, his top straining around his waist-line. The napkin was stained with various sauces and so was his face, orange marks of God knows what right were up past his nose and glimmered with stickiness. He wore a baseball cap and was speaking very loudly, showing everything in his mouth. The rest of his family didn't seem to be eating very much of what was there at all, it all seemed to be his. Not that I could see him surrendering any of it for them. We watched as his fork plunged into at least a dozen plates and made the journey to his mouth and the front of his t-shirt. There were only three people, but they were on a table for six to accommodate all the food and drinks. He was led back in his chair with his legs outstretched, belching and laughing continuously. His poor wife had embarrassment written all over her face as she tried to stack all the plates without drawing any more attention to the table.

After a long day of riding my legs and back were absolutely killing me. We went back to the hotel to spend our last night chilling out, literally as our muscles were throbbing. We aren't really an active family, well not in this league. So it hit us hard after today. We had already eaten so we could just spend the time resting and watching television. We're checking out at around dinner time tomorrow so I'm getting up early to go shopping before we leave. I haven't had chance to go shopping since we've been in San Francisco so I'm going to use tomorrow to go and not have any distractions from Hannah. I've heard it is really good for shopping, and we haven't really done any so I'm excited. We are renting a car tomorrow and will be doing everything for the rest of the holiday via that. It'll be fun to drive to Carmel rather than fly as you get to see different sites and views that you can't experience in the air. And we can stop and start whenever we like. Apart from cabs, we haven't had our own car on this trip, which is rare. We will be on our own with no help; I'm just praying there's a sat nav because it's a long way to go. The rest of the trip will be like this from now on: car journeys. Until we get back to LA to fly home in a few days. I'm looking forward to some retail therapy, though I won't be able to enjoy it unless I rest tonight, I'm aching so badly. Sleep it is now, ready to spend in the morning.

Day Ten – August 27th

This afternoon, we said our goodbyes to San Francisco. I got up extra

early this morning to go shopping on the high street around the corner,

and went into shops such as Forever 21, Abercrombie and Fitch and Old

Navy. We had walked down this street a few times over the last day or

so, and every time I was told, "We'll come back here before we go." This

sentence usually means we won't unless I make it happen. So I took it

upon myself to go without everyone so I could enjoy looking around in

peace. This area was known as Market Street, and was home to the

subway we had come here on a few days before. It was nice not to have a constant whining at my side that I was taking too long; I was free for a little while.

I left the hotel on a pretty empty stomach in order to have more time before my family woke up. I passed the large storage shop "Contain Yourself" on my left; this was my landmark for getting back. It was a huge building, so there was no way I could walk by and not spot it. I followed the road around to the left until I found the shops and places I recognised. The streets were rather sparse, hardly any traffic or people about, which seemed unusual for a Friday morning. Though I suppose I'd missed the original 8am rush. The sky was grey as per usual, and San Francisco was just coming to life.

I walked up to Abercrombie, only to realise it didn't open for another fifteen minutes. I milled about on the empty sidewalk for a while before heading over for a gander around Forever 21, which I could see already had its doors open. It was placed on a corner, and had large silver characters spelling out the name and a flag on the front. It was immediately obvious to me that this was too nice a building to be a shop. It was far too business-like. It had a vast amount of windows;

most were arched whilst some square ones filled in the gaps. The windows around the side each had a letter on the glass, spelling out Forever 21. They were deeply set into the stone walls and were framed in black, and the entrance was placed on the corner of the street. The inside had a very high ceiling, to accommodate both the downstairs and the upstairs floors. There was a row of chandeliers hanging from the dark ceiling to within 6ft of the customer's heads. The floor was immaculate white tiles and led to a transparent staircase edged in fairy lights. Clothes hung from rails, lay folded up on tables and accessories were dotted around in many luminous containers in the shape of crosses. Necklaces and scarves were mounted on the walls, and there was a whole side devoted to them surrounded by more lighting and mirrors. The upstairs had stacks of shoes and some children's clothes, though it wasn't on such a huge scale. It did give a clear view of the downstairs and the people bustling about, and you could see out of the many windows onto the main street. I knew Hannah would want a quick look in here later, so I gave it a once over before heading back across to Abercrombie.

I got back to find people starting to gather outside its doors. As a fellow shop worker, there is nothing more annoying than having people queuing up outside your doors at ungodly hours waiting to come in. It is pressurising, and above all it's very unsettling. Haven't they got homes to go to? Beds to be sleeping in? They stand an inch from the glass breathing on the window, hands arched over their eyes so they can get a good look inside. The watch tapping is my personal hate, as well as eye rollers. It annoys me a great deal, but today I was that person.

I had a good look around inside and visited the surrounding shops before time was starting to get on. I decided a quick peek in Juicy Couture wouldn't hurt either, until I saw that even with a sale on it was way out of my price range. The streets were still pretty quiet by this time, so before heading back I went into an entrance of some kind of mall.

Behind the glass doorways were "coming soon" signs and the sight of many crisscrossing escalators. The ups crossed with the downs and passed each other right up to what looked like the roof. Above them was a mosaic ceiling of many colours piecing together random shapes. I didn't have time to visit all the shops that lined the tile walkways; I had just come to "suss it out" as Mum would say.

"Excuse me miss."

I looked up to see I was being approached by a woman in a white coat from a health and beauty stall. She'd got me. I let her do her rehearsed speech on me and I tuned in and out.

"Do you have a moment? I'd like to show you something amazing."

"Um, OK sure."

"This is from our latest range. This scrub contains salt..."

Blah blah blah. She was going on for ages. It got to the point where I could just see a mouth moving and a hand caressing a bottle. Suddenly she picked up my arm and started to point to it.

"Look, I'll show you." She was smiling, so I just let her show me what she was so desperate to do.

"Smells nice." I was just making polite conversation. She was practically scouring my arm.

"Very nice yes. It removes underlying dirt from your skin that normal soaps don't."

I nodded along, smiling and looking interested.

"Where are you from?" she asked.

"Wales." I waited for the confused look and the questions, but they didn't come.

"Oh lovely," she picked up a sponge to wipe off the scrub.

She ran the sponge along where she had been cleansing, and a brown substance started coming off me. I was baffled that something so gross was clearly embedded in my skin.

"Oh dear, look at this." She was tutting now whilst looking quite pleased with herself. "Don't they have showers in the UK?"

I snatched my arm from her and gave a half-hearted laugh. Cheeky cow. She was looking at me, and I knew what was coming next.

"It's just $29.95 on special offer." She was waiting, expecting me to just give her the money I had brought. I felt myself getting a little panicky.

She watched my face go red and started to get arsey. "How old are you?"

"Fifteen," I lied. "I'll go back and get my mum and bring her up here."

"Well you obviously came out on your own."

"Yes, but I don't have any money."

"So you came out shopping on your own without any money? Is that what you're saying?"

I could feel her anger as her face tensed. Her pupils were enlarging and her hands were fidgety.

"Look, I'll go and get my mum."

I walked away before she could say anything else, stroking my new soft arm. I mean, what if I was fifteen? I wouldn't have that kind of money to flit away on a body scrub. And she approached *me;* I had every right to refuse.

I left the mall sharpish after the incident, and went back to get my family who I knew wanted to go in a couple of shops before leaving. They were ready, bags packed and waiting in the lobby to go around the streets for the last time.

It was really cold and cloudy, but the sky wasn't dark enough for it to rain. The wind was sharp, and sliced into your face like when you bite

into an ice cream. We were all red nosed and red faced by the time we
spotted the Levi's sign in the distance.

"There it is," I said proudly, as I'd spotted it when I was out earlier.

We walked right up to the sodding sign to find a massive "WE HAVE
MOVED TO..." banner plastered across the window. No good when
you're in a place where you don't know where anything is, it put us back
a little.

"We passed one yesterday," said Dad. "Up that way, bigger than this."

A few minutes later and up a side street and we had reached the
desired premises. Everything inside was panelled in wood, the tables,
the floor, the doors and the entire decor. The only reason we had come
to this jean fest was to get some for Hannah. But it was really overly
expensive, much more than we had originally planned. And she was too
small for any of the sizes. We all laughed as she appeared time after
time in ridiculously baggy jeans.

"You should try Macy's," said the sales girl. "They have more
children's sizes."

"Thank you, we'll do that."

To get to Macy's we had to cut through the mall I had encountered earlier. We stopped at Forever 21 and Abercrombie along the way for Hannah to have a look, and then made for the mall. As we passed through, I was telling Mum about the sales assistant from this morning.

"There she is!" I ducked behind Hannah and hurried them past. Luckily she was too busy harassing somebody else at the time to notice. Hopefully we wouldn't come this way on the way back.

On the other side of the mall, the sidewalk was blocked as it was cornered off following an accident that had only happened within the last ten minutes. One car had gone into the back of another at a junction, and a Chinese man was being carried off on a stretcher wearing a neck brace. A fire engine was just pulling up to help and police were desperately trying to pull nosey pedestrians away from the scene whilst taping off the area.

Macy's was too enormous to even comprehend having a look around it in the time we had. We headed straight to the Levi's section, which we identified by the pairs of jeans hanging from the ceiling. The prices here were twice as cheap as the Levi's store we had just been too, so we all decided to have a pair.

"These are for *children?*" Mum was shocked. "They are all enormous! These would fit me!"

We all got away with buying a children's size, even Dad. It was nice and quiet so we each tried on a few pairs before choosing the ones we were going to take home. By filling out a questionnaire at the till we got an extra 10% off the purchases. You can't ask for better than that. They all have "Levi's San Francisco" on the buttons, so I'll always remember where I got them from.

Hannah could quite happily have wandered around in Macy's all day, but we had to go back to the hotel and check out. The concierges had kept our entire luggage in a room in the lobby, for a small fee of course, so it was all ready for us to head back and go. And it was time to see the courtesy car we were getting.

The hotel had upgraded us to a "large family car" which we anticipated would be much too large for us.

"We are getting something called a Chrysler?" said Mum.

"What?! Really?" I like Chryslers and was excited at the thought of having one.

"Here's the key to the car sir, have a good trip." The concierge handed over the key to Dad and pointed us in the direction of a large car.

"That's not a Chrysler." I was most disappointed. Instead, we had been given a 4x4. A Chevrolet Traverse. Don't get me wrong, it was a good car, massive boot and seats and with loads of features. Including a Sat Nav, thank god. We left the car park and drove out into the sunlight that was starting to appear, before pulling into a lay-by outside to get our bearings and to set up the Sat Nav. This is where the first problem started.

"I can't find my glasses," said Dad, the designated driver.

"They can't be far, check the bags."

Minutes later and all the bags had been rifled through. No glasses.

"Maybe I left them in the room. Go back and look before they start cleaning it."

Mum left the car and set off in search of someone who could look in the room for us.

Meanwhile, in the car, a traffic warden leaning against the hotel was giving us daggers. We were on his territory, parked in a loading bay and had been stationary for some time now. He eventually gave in and came over and tapped on the window.

"Excuse me sir, you can't stop here indefinitely."

"Yes I know, it'll just be another few minutes. I'm just waiting for my wife, she's forgotten something."

Hannah and I looked at each other and couldn't help but laugh.

The warden shook his head and began backing away, returning to his spot against the wall. He was keeping his eyes firmly fixed on us, bowing his hat over his eyes to try and hide the fact he was staring at us. All he needed was to be flipping a coin to complete the image. Then Mum appeared and got back into the car.

"They aren't there. They checked everything."

"Great. By the time we get there it'll be getting dark and I won't be able to read the signs properly. Right, well you'll have to take over if need be."

Mum gulped, really not comfortable with the concept of six lane traffic in another country.

"Well we may have no choice." He sensed her panic.

"We'll see how it goes."

It was just under two hours to drive to Carmel-on-sea. We had a Sat Nav, but other than that we had no idea. A two hour drive through California along dusty motorways and coastal roads, there was always something to focus your attention on. Whether it was the sheriff doing his rounds on his motorbike, or being flipped off by road ragers who are fed up of tourist's faffing on their roads. The sea out of my window was teal and rippled into darker shades the closer to the horizon it got. The sand was white and fine and blew effortlessly forming little piles on the sides of the road. The sky remained cloudless and the roads were uneven and bumpy. The tarmac was pale and filled with angry drivers ready to give you a hard time for being in the wrong lane. It was easy to doze off with my headphones in, but I was awoken by Hannah being sick into a bag next to me. Neither of us is very good on long car journeys.

I woke up briefly a few times to see groups of trees sheltering the road and open green fields alongside us. The greenery didn't last long as we came back out into the open with views right across the water. Only a crash barrier separated us from large sandbanks and the sheet of blue that lay beside us. The sky was completely free from blemishes and the sea rippled silently whilst sparkling under the sunlight. The sight looked as though it could never end, but it soon did for us as we entered through more hillside areas and along the winding roads approaching the town. I was proud of myself for doing so well in the car for such a long time, but when you're surrounded by such beautiful views you remain pretty much occupied. The scenes of natural beauty may be something that Californians take for granted, but they are something I will never forget.

The next time I woke up we were weaving through the residential streets of Carmel. We arrived at Hofsas House hotel just uphill from the beach and situated on the busiest road we were going to see here.

Traffic and noise is virtually nonexistent a lot of the time. Dad manoeuvred the car downhill under a low arch and into the tightly packed car park with only a few spaces. The headroom above the ramp wasn't very high, and it was touch and go whether the Chevy would get down there without scraping itself either on the roof or the ground. The hotel was bright pink and was on a very small scale. The reception had a log fire and a few wicker chairs, and had a Bavarian style decor inside and out. It doubled up as a place to collect your breakfast from and take back upstairs, so the selection in the mornings was always very little. The stairs led to a long open balcony that looked out at the sea, and had the entrance to each room on it. It also had a table and chairs at the end of it for you to eat your breakfast outside.

We had room 46. Inside there were two massive double beds with brass headboards and yellow floral duvets. Each bed had a lamp above it and was made with pastel sheets. We also had an open plan kitchen and a TV to watch from the bed, and a dressing table by the window with a chair and a large lamp. The bathroom was long and narrow with a big shower, a few counters and a cupboard for towels and a hairdryer. It was the epitome of adorable.

The whole town is on a tiny scale. The beach is the main attraction, and is surrounded by lots of similar cottage style hotels. It is a dog's dream, the one's on the beach were so happy and content with running up and down with sticks for hours. There were specific hotels that allowed them to stay, and had areas for them to hide away out of the heat.   There is a selection of shops and eateries about, mostly souvenirs and antique type stores. It's a beautiful place, but I don't understand how people could stay here indefinitely and not get bored. I suppose it's more of a retirement town. The outside of most buildings are masked in creeping vines and flowers on the beams that cling to the sides. Everything is stripped back to basics, and the residents are happy with this. Carmel is also known for several unusual laws, including a prohibition on wearing high-heel shoes without a permit, enacted to prevent lawsuits arising from tripping accidents caused by irregular pavements.

The sun was setting over the sea as we walked down the beach, creating streaks of light amongst the waves. There were small cliffs either side of the sand that accommodated small wooden houses and grass verges and woodland. It was as we headed back through the town we realised that they don't have any streetlights here. Unwilling to see their village become "citified," Carmel's founding fathers rejected the practice of house-to-house mail delivery in favour of a central post office. To this day, there are still no addresses, parking meters or street lights, and no sidewalks outside of Carmel's downtown commercial area. The seaside European style town is only one square mile so everything is within walking distance. And it is rated the "Number 7 City Destination in the United States" by Condé Nast Traveler.

With celebrities such as Clint Eastwood and Joan Fontaine living in Carmel, it hardly made news when ardent animal lover/actress Doris Day purchased part ownership in the historic Cypress Inn. Her love for animals has given Carmel the reputation of being a "dog's heaven" and allowed so many of the hotels to allocate specific rooms for owners to stay with them. Due to its small and intimate layout, since 2010,

141

Carmel-by-the-Sea's population is only 3,938 people. Because of its exclusivity, compared to the rest of the country the cost of living is 101.40% Higher than the U.S. average.

I hope tomorrow will be a lot warmer than today, though it is already a lot warmer than San Francisco. The wind is smoother and warm, but it's still jacket weather. After queuing we ate in a little bar called "Aw Shucks" (the only decently priced place we could find anywhere) which was cute even if it was rather cramped. It was small and each table was only an arm's length away, all the walls we mirrored and the lighting was sparse.

We headed back to the hotel using the lights from surrounding homes and businesses. Mum and Dad decided to stay out, so Hannah and I walked back and experienced all this together. We are supposed to be going to the beach and to explore tomorrow, but I've got a feeling we've seen pretty much all there is already, and we've only been here one evening. All I want is to have the heat back, and having a decent tan to go home with. So fingers crossed for tomorrow, especially now I've spotted the hotel pool directly below our room. Let the tanning

commence.

Day Eleven – August 28th

First and last day in Carmel and I'm not too sad to see it go. It's a beautiful place, but it's too quiet and timid, and too secluded. For me, I enjoy the sleepy beach town as much as the next person, but there's a limit. There is only so much lack of activity I can endure at one time, especially when the weather isn't all that spectacular.

Mum and I were up early, and were looking over the balcony at the mist resting on the sea. The day was just starting to brighten up, the wind was getting stronger and the gulls could be heard in the distance.

"Help me bring the breakfast up?"

I nodded.

We headed down to reception to see a small spread of orange juice, toast, a muffin basket and some cereal on a table before us. There were bowls, plates, a dish of fruit and different preserves at the head of the table, as well as a small pile of trays to transport your chosen items to your room. The brickwork around the large log fire glowed as it had already been lit, and the receptionist gave us a nod as we entered and poked at the display, before turning and picking up a ringing phone. I balanced most things in my arms, following Mum back up the stairs to present what we had to the other two, though we were sure they wouldn't be awake yet.

The weather was not up to my expectations at all. It was cloudless yes, and the sun was starting to appear, but it was still very dingy and grey. The sun never really shone to its full capacity, which was a massive let down. In order to get to the reception, we had to make the journey entirely outside. So I made assumptions about the weather very quickly. The rays of sunlight were very weak, and it was definitely not weather for stripping down and lying on a beach. It was cool and we had no way of knowing if it would brighten up later on. The fire in the corner of reception was burning brightly, giving off a strong heat. Not a good sign

of the day ahead.

There wasn't really anything we could do instead.

"Why don't you take Hannah to the shops?"

"There aren't any shops."

"The few we passed yesterday. Oh go on, we'll meet you at the beach

in a bit."

I agreed reluctantly. Now I had to drag three shops out for as long as

possible, maybe including a brief walk would make it last? Then it was

off to sitting on a beach in blustery sea wind.

It turned out that two of the shops had large glass cabinets running

through the middle of them, lined with figurines of every animal you

could think of. Foxes, bear, cats, dogs and birds lined the surface, each

rooted to a wooden base. They were Antique shops. We were the

youngest people around by a clear mile. The far corner of the shops

housed a few postcard stands and some random household gimmicky

items. My favourite was some cats as salt and pepper pots that were

kissing; they looked like my cat at home.

We felt very uncomfortable as we entered. It didn't help that we were drawn attention to by the annoying bells that rang when we opened the door. The old woman behind the counter instantly gave us the "don't touch anything" look, peering over her glasses before going back to cleaning the items. The walls were decorated with portraits of the area past and present, and there was a small map of California stuck by the door with thumbtacks.

"Can we go now?" Hannah hissed in my ear.

"Why? Wait a minute. I want to pick a postcard, give me chance."

"Because she won't stop staring at us."

I chose a card and ignored the fake smile from the owner, leaving quickly with no intention of returning.

Just opposite the shop was the most adorable petrol station that I had ever seen. Sheltered by trees and with just a few pumps, it was all that this small town required. It had a small kiosk at the far end, with a large wooden shell suspended from the wooden beams it was built with. The wooden shell was engraved, and hung swinging back and forth so it was seen clearly from the road. Eight white pillars with wooden roofs were home to the eight pumps, and a small yellow Shell sandwich board was placed at the entrance displaying the prices. It was hardly ever in use in the few times I passed it; just a small local point for refuelling every once in a while was all that was necessary. It was like something out of the Flintstones, but it has been known to have celebrities stop by to fill up from time to time.

Also nearby was a small fire station. A building that was just four fire engines wide made with beige stone and looked anything but what it actually was. There were four sets of red shutters, two open and two closed. Above the shutters was a wooden plaque reading "Carmel-By-The-Sea Fire Station" that was the length of two of the exits. Three sets of windows were above the plaque, and occupied the remaining blank wall on the building. The roof and chimney made it look more like a large house, and even with the two fire engines peering out onto the road it was hard to believe that it was a fire station. Hannah and I sat on a bench opposite and looked at it for a while. The bench was a bus stop, though I am yet to see any buses pass through anywhere. We discussed our next move.

"Where do you want to go now?"

"There's one more shop on the way to the beach I wanted to look in."

This one, thankfully, had clothes. It was a surfer type shop that contained everything you would need for the beach nearby. It was decorated with wood, but in a very different way to the Levi's store in San Francisco. It was purposely left with jagged edges and an uneven surface, like driftwood they had just found on the beach. The changing rooms and tables were the same, and the wall had a surfboard and posters of the sea on it at different times of the year. I bought myself a pair of joggers which read "Carmel Lifeguard" down the left leg. They were supposed to be cropped, so I bought extra large so that they would reach the floor. So at least it wasn't a wasted journey.

En route to the beach, we passed more dogs than people. Wet dogs passed us, shaking and leaving their paw prints on the road. The pavements became dusted with sand the closer we got to the beach, the hotels became further apart and the trees stopped at the bottom of the hill. Cars lined the one side of the road and the beach began to unfold in front of us.

"See if you can spot them," I said.

It wasn't hard. The beach was pretty vacant. There were lots of dog walkers and people passing through, but very few sunbathers. It just wasn't the right weather for it. We found our parents on the rise of sand coming down from the road. They were lying down, eyes shut and oblivious to what was going on around them. Mum even had a cardigan covering most of her face. Even the dogs that were running dangerously close with their sticks and a man playing an accordion on a nearby blanket didn't faze them. He was getting the attention from everyone else who went by, his floppy hat hiding his face and his Hawaiian shirt flapping in the breeze. His wife clapped along and straightened out their blanket. Many people stopped to applaud him and give requests to what he would play next.

The wind was blowing at intervals, but it was still nowhere near warm enough for me to contemplate taking my cardigan off let alone anything else. I looked over at Hannah who looked just as bored as I did, seeing as our parents had barely acknowledged our arrival.

"Finish burying me in the sand?"

I looked closer and Hannah's legs were pretty much gone. She was heaping mounds of sand onto he lap in the hope to ease her boredom, and it kind of took off from there. So I made a start on her torso. The game didn't last very long though, I soon ran out of body and we were back staring into space again within a few minutes.

"Do you want to go in the hotel pool?" I asked.

Her face lit up. "Yes! Come on this is boring."

Mum nodded and rolled over as we left the windy beach.

"Apparently the pool's heated," I said. "It's bloody freezing so I hope it is!"

This was the topic of conversation as we walked back up the hill; anything had to be better than sitting on an open beach and being hit with cold sea air.

Unfortunately, the pool was not what we had built it up to be. We were its only occupants and it was not heated at all. Quite the opposite actually. I felt as though people on the above balcony were judging us

for venturing in, as there was always someone looking at us. I felt like

they were sniggering, watching our every move. Hannah jumped in and

was swimming the perimeter of the circular pool within moments, but I

just couldn't get warm.

"Come and do handstands with me."

"I'm too cold. I'll watch you."

"Well you're not going to get warm sitting on the step!"

I played with her for what seemed like ages and I still was absolutely

freezing. I left her doing laps and began setting her challenges whilst I

sat on the side. I wrapped up in a towel for a while, but as the sun

slowly began to shine brighter I didn't need it as much.

I lay on the mesh sun bed and watched her frolicking about in the

water for a while, but as more people arrived to join her I rolled over

and attempted to relax. We had briefly stopped in a crowded bakery on

the way back, and the cookie I had was making my stomach feel heavy.

Despite that, I couldn't help wondering when we would next be eating.

My stomach had a sharp stinging pain on the outside, and was making me aware it was sore as I was lying on it. Assuming the mesh didn't really agree with me, I tried closing my eyes for a bit.

I was awoken by a dripping shape that was ready to leave.

"I need a shower." She persisted.

I sat up to reveal a very raw stomach, and a very red one. I shrugged it off as we made our way up to the room. It wasn't until I got inside and looked in the mirror that I realised how red I was generally, and also how pink Hannah had gone. Mum will kill me for letting her burn, I thought as we both inspected ourselves in the mirror. I was worse, my stomach was almost blistered and our faces were all blotchy.

"It's not even hot outside!"

"The wind tans you," I said.

My new found sunburn made sitting down very difficult, I just couldn't get comfortable for more than a few moments at a time. Our parents arrived back shortly after to discover our patchy state.

"And why weren't you wearing any cream?"

"Well I was, a bit."

"Look at you both, you're supposed to reapply it."

"It was so windy. We didn't think it was necessary..."

"It's the wind that tans you the most."

"Well I know that now!"

I knew that anyway, but I didn't know it would be this bad. If anything I thought it would look good. It felt stupid reapplying in the cold and wind and Hannah pretty much didn't leave the pool for me to do it anyway. Either way I'll do it next time.

A shower and an after sun session later and we were out for tea at the Hog's Breath restaurant. It is famous for being Clint Eastwood's restaurant before he sold it on, and is somewhere most visitors to Carmel like to visit. It has a large menu for all the different times of the day, and includes meals such as the Dirty Harry Dinner, burger and chilli dog.

Eastwood is a native Californian who discovered the Carmel area during the Korean War when he was stationed at nearby Fort Ord. He eventually returned to Carmel where he still lives. In 1972, a friend was showing him around a building he owned. "Wouldn't this make a great saloon?"he asked. Clint must have agreed because when his friend left town, he bought the building and made into the now legendary Hog's Breath.

In 1986, when he wanted to expand the building, he got bogged down in Carmel's notorious red tape. So he ran for Mayor and won by a 72% landslide. In his two years as Mayor he got sidewalks put in on the downtown streets, an annex built for the library and his building enlarged. The Hog's Breath closed in 1999 and then re-opened under new management.

The inside is warm and cosy and is the perfect haven from a cold night. Not that they have too many of those, well not seriously cold anyway. There are open stone fires spread around the place and the walls looked like varnished floorboards. The tables and chairs were nondescript and functional, and there was a large hog's head mounted on the wall both inside and out. The walls were covered in photos of Clint Eastwood, and the layout reflected his personality. As well as portraying scenes from his films. This included a black and white shot of him pointing a gun up close, which when Dad sat below it looked like it was shooting him in the head.

The outside was far more beautiful. A large patio hidden around the back of the restaurant was sheltered by overhanging trees. There were plenty of benches as logs made into tables, as well as being outlined with fairy lights and yet more fireplaces. All the furniture was misshapen, varnished and the edges smoothed over. They were supposed to look jagged, fresh from the forest floor so to speak, with as little modification as possible. There was an outdoor bar and lots of people bustling about; it gave the scene a snug feel. As you come down the steps, there is a large wall in front of you which is the building next door. The wall has been painted as a landscape, complete with blue sky and the image of fields and mountains trailing off into the distance. The greens lifted right off the backdrop and lighten up the entire place, and appear very real when glancing passed.

It was easy for time to get away when sitting in such a warm environment, but finally Hannah and I left and headed back to the hotel. We watched *Forrest Gump* as we packed, before settling down ready to go to sleep. It was fun to watch the film after being in its themed restaurant only a few nights ago, and it reminded me of scenes I had long since forgotten.

Day Twelve – August 29th

Awakening to another dreary day, Mum and I set about the breakfast collecting ritual once again. The fire in the lobby was burning brightly and was sparking onto the rug, a sign of the day that was to be expected. The mist was hanging in the air and the silence was deafening. It was half past ten, and I was more than ready to move onto Santa Barbara.

The four hour drive took up a lot of the day, and we were once again back on the freeways of California. As it was the furthest car journey of the trip so far, Hannah was instructed to sit in the front.

"I'm not having you being sick again."

"I won't be! I promise."

"All the same, I'll feel a lot better if you sit there instead."

After some pouting, we were off and speeding towards a place where the sand burns your toes and even the blasts of sea breeze sizzle. She did very well actually. As we passed by some similar scenery and through some towns, she fell asleep with her Ipod in.

"Best thing for her to do really," said Mum.

Dad was messing around with the radio stations, swerving along the roads as he did so. The longer we stayed in the car, the more stations came in and out of range. Seeing as we had no idea about regions, there was no telling how long a station would be with us. Just when a song we liked came on, the channel was lost. None of us had thought about bringing any CDs with us. Why should we? Nobody just carries CDs around anymore. It's like asking me if my phone has an aerial or I still use my video player. Without my once popular walkman, there never seemed a reason to have them nearby.

"We'll keep this one on for now," said Dad.

"What is it?"

"I don't know, a Latino station or something."

"It's quite catchy actually."

The radio station reminded me of a trip we had taken to Portugal some time ago now. Back when I was blonde and Hannah was still cute.

We were driving around with the same CD playing for the full two weeks; we were in the car much more than anticipated. Coincidently, it was also a Latino mix. Vibrant and fun to listen too, making you want to get up and dance. Even if I couldn't understand a lot of the words.

The journey was restless and seemed to drag. I was starving, and there were only so many times I could repeat staring out of the window, snoozing and listening to my ipod. Being a bad traveller, I limit myself. Reading or playing on a phone/device is out of the question. Well, unless I wanted to risk something unpleasant happening to the back of Hannah's head.

Mum was constantly dozing; Dad was concentrating on his surroundings and from what I could see Hannah was out for the count. The seat in front of me was so large it was impossible to see any part of her. I could see a gormless sunglass-wearing face in the passenger mirror slumped right down, so I guessed that was my answer.

The hotel we were heading for was supposed to be very luxurious. Don't get me wrong, I really liked Hofsas House, despite there being nothing around to do. But the Fess Parker Resort was promised to be very different. And by that I mean something to actually do.

It was very confusing I'll tell you that much. The Sat Nav led us into the site of the resort at around half two. It was easy to spot from the road, as there was a group of high white flagpoles flying many hotel flags at the entrance. Here, being us, we hit a problem. In order to get into the grounds there was a barrier in place. The two cars ahead of us got in without a hitch, but the damn thing refused to lift for us.

Dad manoeuvred back and forth hoping the sensor would suddenly realise we were there. No joy. The queue was snaking back behind us until it reached the road. There was no indication of the barrier lifting anytime soon; no matter how many times Dad hit the button in temper. He faffed with the ticket dispenser before swallowing his pride and pressing the help button, a jolly voice was on the other end. One palaver later, and we finally on our way.

Into the maze of the hotel we went, a large car park panned out before us and a golf course lay behind a high white wall, buggies of wild players in spotless baseball caps and checked shorts cutting us up at every turn. The entrance itself was very extravagant. There was a paved driveway with a circle of greenery at its centre and everywhere was decorated with palm trees. Drivers were circling the area and were met by concierges ready to assist with your luggage. The doors were sheltered under a smooth white tunnel with a slated caramel roof. Three arches were displayed in front of us; the largest indicated the main entry point and the others merely decorative. Flowers decorated the roots of the palms trees as they rested on the white wall, and benches were scattered about and various lanterns attached themselves wherever they could. The doors themselves were also arched, the glass above them was edged in thick black paint and the arches became smaller and smaller until a small set of doors was in sight. There was always someone to hold them open for you, armed with a smile, though of course they expected a tip.

To the side of the paved forecourt was a large wall that led to the pool area. I was absolutely desperate to use the toilet, after being trapped in a car for four hours. My family, however, just strode off ready to explore. I assured myself that the pool must have toilets, and followed them through a sort of passage underneath the hotel to get to the pool area that was clearly close by. We could hear the splashing and squealing very clearly. The two floors of the hotel were suspended above us, lifts lay to the left of me and there were some toilets on the right. Unfortunately, they needed a key card in order to access them.

I must have had desperation written all over me. Dancing around like a fool with nobody around me, trying out a door that blatantly wasn't going to open. Even after my third, fourth and fifth attempts at it.

"You need to use the toilet, honey?"

I spun around to find a strange woman in a swimming costume and towel smiling at me.

"Yeah," I blushed. "We haven't got our card yet so..."

"Here, use mine." She pushed the card into the slot on the door and a green light lit up. The door open and I was free to enter.

"Thank you so much!" I smiled not wanting to seem rude and ungrateful, but I truly couldn't wait any longer. I think she got the message though, and she and her flowery beach towel were nowhere to be found when I reappeared.

I don't think I've ever been so happy to see a toilet.

The pool was much larger than the one in Carmel, and its corners were indented to make seating areas at each end, outlined with darker tiles. It was bustling with lots of guests, sun beds and cabanas and was a totally different atmosphere. The whole area was guarded with card access only, but we could see a bar at the side and plenty of greenery and palm trees in the surrounding area. Though it would have been pretty easy to jump the fence had we wanted too. We lent onto a black fence that sealed the pool in, and noticed to the left we could access the street from here. I felt the sensation of thick grass brushing the bottom of my feet and blades peering between my toes. It was time to enjoy some sun.

Finally we had the hot and sticky heat we had been craving for so long. And pavements you could cook burgers on.

"I'm starving," I blurted out.

"I'm sure there is some chocolate and bits in one of the bags."

"I hope so. We've had no dinner and I'm really hungry."

"I know that, it's the same for all of us. Like I said, check Dad's bag."

We went back to the car to collect everything, eager to get back into

the heat before it began to relax and the breeze appeared. The

concierges were ready to pounce as we crossed the driveway and made

our way towards the arches. The men eagerly tried to snatch things

from our grasp.

"We are fine thank you." Dad smiled.

They stood back and nodded. They must get rejection tens of times a

day, and I'm sure not all of them are so polite. One still insisted on

holding the door open for us. Mum was struggling with one of the cases

so another stepped in to help. She smiled and thanked him; he smiled

back. Though I think he was hoping for a little more than that.

When we checked in, we each received a complimentary cookie as a

welcome to the hotel. It was still hot and was presented in a white

paper bag, the chocolate chips smeared against the inside, and it wasn't

long before my fingers were in the same state. We dumped our luggage

in room 218, barely stopping to take in how attractive it was. Two

double beds made up in green and yellow checked bedding with leather

ottomans at the foot. Each side had large white pillows which read

"Sweet Dreams" and a solid wooden headboard supported them upright to stop them from falling. There was a wardrobe, a full length mirror and a dressing table all made of wood, and a passage leading to the bathroom provided another storage space and dressing table. There was another mirror with lights and the dresser had drawers and a hairdryer tucked into a drawstring bag. Everything was large and chunky, much bigger than average furniture. It was all ready to be laden with our things.

We had a balcony, which two large glass doors slid to reveal. It had a table and chairs and a tiled floor, and overlooked the pool and the other areas of the hotel on the other side. It was like a mini village, complete with little fences and perfectly clipped bushes. We could also see the road that led to the beach, and the sea glistening in the sun like glitter on a pane of glass. The sky was clear and the street and grass were dotted with palm trees. I was more than ready to hit the pool.

"Don't you think you should be covering up your stomach?"

"We go home in two days. I'm making the most of it."

"You don't want it getting any worse than it already is, blistering even."

"It'll be fine. It's got cream on it. I can worry about it getting better when we get home."

She frowned at me and whipped out a magazine. Mum very rarely ventures into the pool whenever we go away, she just likes to relax and judges from the side. I like to do both. As I've gotten older, I find spending hours in the pool rather tedious, and prefer to read on the side. I guess I've just gone past the hand standing and retrieving things from the bottom phase, the one where time used to be gone before you knew it. Now it just made it drag. Plus the cold water hitting my stomach in waves from all the movement wasn't my idea of a good time.

We were some of the last people to leave the pool, and even though it was still pretty hot the sun was dimming fast. Mum and Dad enjoyed a drink at the bar whilst I looked on in envy. It was time I took a shower ready for the evening anyway.

As much as I was already getting into the Santa Barbara life, as soon as the sun went down we realised we weren't really within walking distance of anything. A flaw in what seemed to be a perfect place. There was a pier within sight, but when we began to walk towards it we soon saw it was a lot further than anticipated. When we finally got to it, there was a mini fair lit up at the end of it. The area was blocked off, so we didn't even get a proper look at what was going on. Surprisingly, there were hardly any people about and aside from the lights of the fair, not many streetlamps lit up the beach and walkway. The small buildings opposite the pier were almost all in darkness. We were far from what seemed like everywhere. It was like being in a Wild West ghost town; all it needed was the tumbleweeds.

"So where are we going to eat?" Hannah whined.

"There will be something somewhere, a hotel as big as that with nothing around it seems a bit odd to me."

We wandered aimlessly in the empty street for a while; my stomach howling with every step. It was a main road, yet I could count the amounts of cars we saw on one hand. Then a restaurant with its lights on came into view. "Eladio's" was a small and quiet place, expensive too. But it was the only building in sight that had any lights on. It didn't have many customers so we were seated and served right away. The outdoor area was scarce, despite having squashy chairs and patio heaters for the breezy nights. The inside was just a bar, a big screen TV and a cluster of tables. It was a quaint atmosphere, and our waiter was very friendly and glad of our custom. I expected it to be much busier, especially as there wasn't anywhere else to choose from. My steak was tasty and filling. Everyone seemed to be enjoying themselves. It was so peculiar that there was hardly anyone here. Where were all the people?

Not sure of how to get back, we ended up cutting through another resort. It was almost pitch black as we fought through trees and bushes with almost nobody around. It's a wonder we didn't set any sprinklers off. We just strode on, hoping for the best and that we would come out into familiar territory. We did see a large amount of hobos, cocooned in their sleeping bags and resting on various private resort benches. Hidden in the dark and shrubbery, no one would ever know they were here. They were all surrounded by lots of belongings in black bags and didn't move as we walked by. I jumped as every so often one of them grunted, which is scary when you can't always see them, and when you are in a strange place. I suppose there are much worse places to be homeless than a beach in California.

We burst through some bushes and into the grounds of Fess Parker. The lights from the hotel cascaded across the lawns, illuminating the sprinklers and giving one side of each palm tree an orange glow. We followed the beams of light across the thick grass and entered the lobby through a side door, and took the stairs to our floor.

On the way through the corridors of the hotel, Hannah filled up an ice bucket for me to put on my stomach. The burning sensation was worse, and I was very grateful for something to put on it.

I ended up scurrying about in the middle of the night filling a flannel with ice cubes just to try and make myself comfortable. It was already dragging, so I settled down and strategically placed the parcel on my stomach and made the best of a bad situation.

Day Thirteen – August 30th

After a very strenuous few weeks, today was going to be one of the relaxing days that we had done so very few of this holiday. Nothing too exhilarating, just stretched out by the pool and sleeping on the beach, activities which involved as little movement as possible. Well that was the plan. Firstly though, we began the day with a hotel breakfast.

You'll remember me saying on more than one occasion that this had never been a particularly important part of the day for us. Rushed Starbucks here and there and carrying tray loads of snacks up to the room for consumption was not really a good way to start any day. But this morning was very different; we were eating downstairs with a wide selection of food, a bit like what we had in LA almost two weeks ago. Breakfast is always said to be the most important meal of the day, but this one exceeded that description in so many ways.

At the far side of the lobby, counters were pushed against the glass of the windows overlooking the sea. Then opposite they were against a waist-high barrier separating the food area from the seating. The whole area was filled with booths, tables and chairs, and by 10am when we arrived there weren't many people still left eating. We pretty much had the waiter's full attention.

"Here's some orange juice, please help yourself to the buffet."

And that we did.

Hannah was up and away with a large plate and I wasn't far behind her. There was a large four-tiered black stand with glass shelves stacked with drinking glasses. Each glass was topped up with fruit. Each variety of melon was diced into a container, and colour coordinated onto each shelf. The yellow housing two shelves. Next to them on each side was a long glass shelf supported at each end by a silver post. On them were wine glasses, filled with what looked like yogurt and decorated with strawberries.

Behind us were the hot silver platters containing the ingredients for a cooked breakfast. There were sausages, mushrooms, bacon, eggs, tomatoes and more simmering away in their own juices under the lids. To the side was a large milk jug, surrounded by others containing lots of different cereals, as well as a silver fruit bowl. There was a dish of croissants and pastries with various preservatives decorated around the outside in a zigzag fashion. Lastly, next to the coffee maker was a platter of salmon, salad and other slivers of raw fish. It was impossible to not find at least something to have.

"What are you doing?"

Mum was looking very shifty; her napkin was open on her lap and was half covered by the tablecloth.

"What? We have paid for it."

"But what are you actually doing?"

"Making up some sandwiches and bits for the beach later, lunch is sorted then. Pass over your napkin."

I rolled my eyes and handed it over. She was making salmon and salad sandwiches, and was waving frantically over to Dad at the coffee machine to bring over some more bread. He ignored her signals, waving her off and pretending not to know what she was saying.

The windows at the back of the hotel overlooked a sort of coliseum, no roof and arches every foot or so. Every other arch was a window, and trees were placed between each one to brighten up the cream walls. The floor was tiled brown, and could be accessed through steps just along from where we were. Just a door over from where we had entered last night. We were yet to walk through it, but each time we passed it there were groups of excitable children running the perimeter or having races from one side to the other.

Directly across the road was the beach. Which, despite the scorching conditions and it being a Friday in the summer holidays was very much deserted. Much like this area in general. We set up camp almost exactly opposite the coliseum, and now we were a sufficient distance away could see it as a whole. It looked like a wedge of cheese with holes in, especially because of its colour. Behind it was a vast range of mountains. They were dark blue in colour, and the cloudless sky seemed to rest on top of them. You could almost see the peaks sizzling in the heat and the trees at the top gasping for water. The two shades of blue attempted to blend together creating a haze in which the waves of heat could actually be seen. Palm trees were blocking a lot of the hotel, so after gawping at the mountains our attention was quickly brought back to the beach and sunbathing.

No matter where we are in the world, Dad likes to do a lengthy tour of the beach to familiarise himself with his surroundings. Sometimes the process can last a good hour or so. Pacing up and down, venturing so far that he becomes a speck if not less in the distance. He usually likes to go for a swim, but that wasn't really an option with all the shark warnings posted around. Many sharks are spotted in this area and that's as good a reason as any to stay out of the sea.

We discussed heading down to the shopping street later, where lots of well known stores were situated. But that would be after a good dose of lazy time in the sun. After some time had passed though, my headphones were making my ears ache. Everyone around me had their eyes shut, so I carefully shifted onto my elbows for a look around.

Out of the blue, behind us was a lone heron was walking just a few feet away. It looked quite out of place on the beach, but seemed very content with walking up and down. It moved slowly, making prints of broken snowflakes in the hot sand. It took off, flying down gracefully to the pier before beginning its journey back up again.

"Mum. Mum, look..."

Mum absolutely hates birds. They really scare her, always have. Ever since watching the Hitchcock film she's never been able to look at them the same. The bigger they are the worse the problem, but as long as they keep a good distance she's OK. But this heron seemed to be very unpredictable.

"What am I looking at?"

"Over there, look..."

She gasped, sitting bolt upright and disturbing everyone else on the towel, sending sand flying into every ripple. She drew her knees up to her chest and hugged them tightly. Her eyes didn't leave the heron for a second.

He was harmless. Not even flinching when some hobos in a ditch near the road moved under their noisy scratchy sleeping bag.

The heron took off again. Mum shielded her eyes as it flew above us. Outstretched and soaring higher and higher, it was like a small silver plane circling a runway. It flew above some pelicans hovering nearby, which thankfully had no intention of coming our way. They are far too ugly and nosy for my liking.

We stayed on the sand for a little while longer, but the relaxing atmosphere had clearly been lost. We were all restless, so decided now was the time to embark on the shopping trip. After last night's excursion, we already knew that the shops weren't that close by. The hotel had mentioned a sort of shuttle bus that went back and forth every half an hour.

"We'll walk it," said Dad. "Isn't that far and the weather's too good to be on some bus."

It wasn't a bus. More like a glorified golf buggy. One which wanted a pretty hefty fee for an apparently short trip, we discovered by looking at the leaflet.

"I'm happy to walk," I said. So Hannah and I strode off ahead.

"Don't you think you should put your t-shirt back on? You've had that burn exposed all morning."

Not this again.

"I will when we get to the shops."

I led the way, walking along the seafront path in the direction I had seen a shuttle going earlier.

"The receptionist said it's about twenty minutes."

We nodded and walked on. The path had a yellow stripe down its centre like a road, so that people wouldn't clash when walking in different directions. There were far more cyclists, skaters and roller bladers than pedestrians, so you were always a nuisance to somebody. There were large groups of runners and plenty of dog walkers so the path was constantly busy. I was overtaken many times by impatient people on bikes, and we ended up being rather far ahead of our parents. We stopped at some beach toilets to re-group.

Palm trees lined the path, but as they became further apart we became a lot more exposed to the breeze. Twists and turns also began to form, and we ended up crossing a small wooden bridge leading over lots of shallow pools and wet sand. Avoiding people became a lot more difficult at this point. Pelicans were basking and bathing beneath us on mounds of sand, squawking messages to one another. I looked back to see Mum recoiling from the sides of the bridge as they paced beneath her. Golf caddy's and a small car park appeared alongside us, and before we knew it we had reached the dolphin fountain which was placed at the foot of the pier.

"That didn't take long. It shouldn't be too far now."

How wrong we were. From here the road spilt off, and we were informed that the right-hand turn was the street we were looking for. But the street seemed to go on forever. Under a bridge and up a slight incline and there were still no recognisable shops in sight. Dad had stayed behind to look at the pier, so we were down to three and totally confused at the lack of things we had been assured were here. Nothing was remotely familiar. It was exhausting and draining, and we had no idea if we were even in the right area. I left Mum and Hannah pondering and headed to a pharmacy to get some travel tablets for the flight home.

It was a very confusing layout inside, and it was rather crowded. The till area was bustling, and badly placed floor stacks obstructed the walkway. I must have done about five laps of the place and still didn't have what I was looking for.

"Anything I can help you with honey?"

"Do you have anything for travel sickness please?"

He didn't look all that sure either. He led me to an aisle and parked me in front of a bay.

"We have these?"

Motion sickness tablets. Were they the same thing? They had various modes of transport on the box, and for three dollars I was willing to give them a go, anything was better than nothing. I thanked him and headed off.

When I got outside, Dad had caught up with us and everyone was sat on a bench outside. They had spotted some familiar shops further down, but first Hannah was begging for a Starbucks. She and Dad slurped away whilst we walked further down the street in the hope of seeing something we wanted. We did.

A few hours and a lot of purchases later and we ended the spree in Macy's. Dad has been hunting for a denim shirt the entire holiday, and has so far had been more than unsuccessful in his search.

"I'm sorry, we don't have any in at the moment."

"OK, thank you." Yet more disappointment.

"Where are you folks from?" The assistant was quite to keen for us not to move on yet, leaning on a clothes rail as if he had all the time in the world for idle chit chat. Well I suppose it wasn't too busy inside at that point.

"Wales."

"Oh lovely, which part?" Did he actually know what Wales was?

"Newport. Where the Ryder Cup is going to be?"

"Yes, yes, I know it. I lived in Cardiff for a while, loved it there."

This wasn't something we had expected to hear. He surprised us all. The conversation went on to discuss golf and went on for a little while, he was keen to have someone to talk to who knew the area well.

Unfortunately, we then missed the 6pm shuttle we had intended to get. We really didn't have the heart to trudge all the way back, especially with all our new found purchases. We had swallowed our pride and decided that the shuttle was a good idea. But now we had missed it. 6pm was the last bus, which we thought was strangely early, especially when the shops weren't even close to closing for the day yet.

So we had no choice but to set off on foot. Hannah was especially reluctant.

Thankfully though, the sun was much less intense and there wasn't the feeling that the top of your head was being frazzled as you walked. Nothing worse than a burnt scalp. It made the walk that little bit more pleasant, even if it wasn't what we had planned to do, and was a rather long way.

As we walked the shadows were expanding and creeping out onto the road like fingers, reaching out to grab the cars as they went by. The light had begun to fade slowly and shades of orange took over the sky as if someone had smeared the inside of a peach on a canvas. I like walking on holiday because you get to experience the sights properly, stopping and starting whenever you want too, no pressure to keep moving. And you get to touch things. You can experience the heat and watch the traffic, wonder at passing pedestrians and look through windows and into buildings.

By this point of the day however after two such exhausting walks and traipsing around shops for hours I wasn't really in the mood to do any of these things. Instead, I tried to ignore the grooves the shopping bags were leaving in my arms and hands and my t-shirt rubbing against my stomach. We were all uncomfortable, sweaty and tired. Then we became hungry, just wanting to go to sleep and not move for the rest of the night.

The thought of going back out to look for somewhere to go for tea was crippling, so we decided to stay and eat in the hotel restaurant. We sat on some high stools and enjoyed quesadillas and burgers whilst reminiscing about our journey so far. It was quiet and peaceful, just what we needed. The staff left us pretty much alone; but were willing to make us whatever we wanted. Handy when Hannah was making faces at what was on offer on the menu.

I'm totally wiped out after today, but we move onto our final destination tomorrow: Marina Del Rey. One night there and it'll be time to go home. The giant circle we have embarked upon over the last fortnight is almost complete.

Day Fourteen – August 31st

We fly home tomorrow. A day of car rides and plane trips all heading towards the final destination, home. We'll be touching down in the UK the morning after next, so this will be the last entry I'll be writing.

We spent this morning travelling to Marina Del Rey, an area of LA close to beaches and the sunny California you see on TV and in films. The atmosphere would be far from the downtown one we had experienced two weeks ago, far more laid back and mellow. One where we were among all the buildings and the hundreds of tourists milling about; where the noise of the fake lifestyle was banged into your body and mind. A reality shows dream, where nothing ever seems like the real world. Now we were in the quieter community, the lazy surfer type areas. The streets and businesses that surrounded Venice Beach.

We were back to the almost forgotten Starbucks breakfasts early on this morning, then a short car trip led us back to the beginning of our cycle.

"Julia, you can come with me and take the car back."

Dad dropped Mum and Hannah off at the small hotel that the Sat Nav had directed us too before swinging back around and onto the main road. Everything was severely spaced out and the streets only held clusters of people here and there. The hotel was what appeared to be all one level, with smooth pastel blue walls and white trim at the corners. The entrance was sheltered by a shiny blue plastic covered arch which read *Foghorn Harbour Inn* in white letters. There was a convenience store next door, whose entrance was in the car park of the hotel, I guess this puts a lot of business their way. It was a rather dark store inside and sold mostly travel items and bits of food and essentials. It was very quiet and all the walkways were cluttered with unopened boxes and crates. The assistant wasn't too happy either.

The car park and the roads were all immaculate, as if they had been laid that very morning. The sky remained clear, with only passing wisps to disturb the serenity.

Dad and I drove across to the Marriott Hotel where we had been instructed to drop off the car. We could see it straight away, and knew it wasn't far to go. We had no idea where we were supposed to go once we arrived, so once we had navigated the one way system we saw the driveway at the entrance and stopped under a canopy. Dad left me with the car in the middle of the driveway whilst he went in search of some guidance, the engine still running. It was very unsettling as many people walked past and gawped, giving me daggers about where we had stopped. I could see a concierge thinking about whether to approach, rocking back and forth on his heels whilst looking around. Thankfully Dad soon reappeared through the revolving doors in front of me, a slip of paper in his hands.

"That was easy. Come on, got everything?"

"There is nothing..."

The rocking guy walked over and Dad distributed the keys into his hand. They gave each other a nod in thanks before we embarked on the short walk back to the *Foghorn*.

It wasn't far, and after navigating our way across busy roads and strange crossings we were back at the hotel. The inside of the hotel was what can only be described as beach-themed. The lobby was decorated with shells and framed paintings made from sand and glitter. There were many wicker chairs and a wicker settee overlooking a small balcony and out into the harbour. The reception desk had a bowl of sweets on the counter, and a Hawaiian lamp of a hula girl had a warm glow around it. I must have helped myself to at least half a bowl. There were book shelves filled with books and DVDs to rent in the evenings and the floor was wooden with scattered rugs. The pastel blue carried on throughout the hallways and was bordered with thick white lines. This area served as the centre of the hotel, as two corridors split from it creating passages to the rooms. Amongst the chairs was a set of spiral stairs surrounded by a rail which led to the downstairs; it held a lot of rooms despite only having two floors, one of them being a breakfast room. The Wi-Fi was also the best we had come across so far, ironic when we are leaving tomorrow.

We were only a twenty minute walk from Venice Beach and the shops which were nearby. The hotel itself had a small beach which was next to the harbour, but wasn't very popular as it didn't catch much sun. A few volleyball nets and the opportunity for some novice sports was about all it had to offer. Our room had a balcony which overlooked the entire scene of the harbour, but the rooms directly below had only a high-walled yard to sit in. They had no privacy as we could look down at their every move, especially as our balcony was glass. They knew they were being watched, but could do nothing about it. We often giggled at the tops of their heads which circled the yard like rabbits in a pen. They certainly wouldn't get very much sun, and the harbour seemed to be murky all the time from what we had seen so far. It was dinner time on our last day.

"To the beach!"

The sun was at its peak, so we set off to the beach saddled with towels, sun cream and ipods for the last time. The sand was spread out in front of us far in both directions, but there weren't really any people here either. There was a bright yellow and red lifeguard station as we entered from the road, and a male lifeguard lurked nearby in his sunglasses and red outfit. A large 4x4 with a red cross on the side patrolled the beach, doing laps of the area and leaving patterns pushed into the sand. There were also some toilets, which considering they were on a celebrity hot-spot were pretty dark and shabby inside. There were no lights, the doors didn't lock and the soap was obsolete. The walls were black and the floor a dark green with a powdery coating. The sand on the floor was dry and flaky, caking my feet and making them itchy.

Mum and Dad began to take a stroll at the water's edge, legs being tickled by the small ripples. Hannah was restless and began poking me in the side.

"Take my picture?"

She posed, looking away to make it look like an unexpected shot. The natural look apparently. She took some of me too, though they just looked like we were deliberately ignoring the camera. We had a few pictures of us from different angles as the sun began to set. When the light begins to drop that little bit, it's like a sign that sunbathing is over for the day as the little people who were around vacated sharply.

We took some final snaps as a family on a wooden walkway by the lifeguard station that jutted out into the sea like a small pier that wasn't quite useful for anything. The shadows were forming and it was time to get out the cardigan I had slipped into my bag. Through the palm trees that made a border around the sand, the sun shot out peach beams as it lowered closer and closer to the ocean. Our time at the beach may not have been as long as we had hoped, but it was enough for a snooze and to catch some final rays for this holiday. Because quite frankly, we have spent so much time walking about we have barely had any time to build up a proper tan. The odd day here and there is all we have had in the way of sunbathing, so we are not as noticeably brown as I'd have liked to have been. But today was a good day, even if Mum was still nagging about my stomach and how I was making it so much worse for myself. Well, at least there was no heron this time.

It's a Saturday night, so despite it only really being late afternoon the bars and clubs were already starting to heat up. Walking back down the main road and many of the bars had their doors flung open, the music blasting, and a selection of people at tables out the front laughing and having a good time. There was a large amount of souvenir shops along both sides of the street, and as usual I felt obliged to go inside. Hannah pretty much insisted, though all I really wanted was a postcard.

"Hurry up, I'm hungry."

"Yeah, all right. Wait a minute, I've waited long enough for you."

"I don't even know where Mum and Dad are."

"Outside somewhere?"

"Well I can't see them."

"Have you even looked?"

My first thought was that they had taken a shine to a bar or something. Why though, I couldn't explain, especially knowing we couldn't get inside and they were the only ones with a room key. Hannah and I patrolled the surrounding shops and curious looking buildings in a bid to amuse ourselves until they came into sight. They reappeared sauntering along just when I was starting to lose patience with the annoying child whining constantly at my side. Plus, some rather dodgy looking characters were starting to appear ready for a good night out. The stereotypes for trouble were beginning to disperse so it was time to think about vacating the area.

We took a stroll back, and were back at the room around half an hour later. It was the last time we would all be sharing a room like this, two double beds within a few feet of each other for two weeks is an effort in itself, especially with all the fidgeting and snoring. This room was a lot smaller than some of the others we had stayed in, and tomorrow we would have to bring our breakfast up here too. It was only for one night though.

A few doors down from the hotel and just over from the convenience store was a Cheesecake Factory. I wasn't enthralled at the prospect of visiting another one of these, especially as I had felt so ill after going to the one in San Francisco. But this one was far from just being one of a chain, it was beautiful. The dark car park was illuminated by the red lettering which was placed up high and reflected on the decking. The inside was a lot less overpowering and the queue for a table was pretty much non-existent. As a whole, I was much more impressed already.

"Would you like to sit outside?"

"Yes please."

We passed the golden-edged cheesecake counter which displayed mouth-watering options which I would most definitely be experiencing later. Outside on the deck, the tables were all placed close together with fairy lights making a web above us. There were patio heaters to keep off the evening chill, which gave a glow to the harbour we now had such a vivid view of. They did become excessively hot after a while, and Mum needed to ask if they could turn it down slightly.

"Are you going to have a cheesecake this time?"

Seeing as I'd missed out the last time. The whole table including the waitress were all looking at me eagerly; she was tapping her notepad with the tip of her pencil.

"I'll have a chocolate one please."

She offered to box up anything we didn't feel we could finish to take away with us, but we politely declined the offer. We foolishly believed that a sliver of cake would be no match for us, but the portion was far larger than we had anticipated. We couldn't finish it. Well not me, Mum or Hannah. Each piece was so rich that it was just too difficult we cope with a large amount of it. Everyone had shared a cake in San Francisco, so had decided this was the opportunity to experience their own. It was an all around bad decision. No matter how good they tasted or how badly you didn't want to waste them it was impossible to clear the plate.

Back at the hotel and the crowded room was now taken over by open suitcases and bags of toiletries. The frantic search for passports and warmer clothes for the plane overshadowed everything; travel tablets and flight socks became a priority. We were ready to leave, but at the same time we weren't. This would be one of the greatest adventures we would ever have, and it was set to end with a hotel microwave and some bad TV.

8732021R00115

Printed in Great Britain
by Amazon.co.uk, Ltd.,
Marston Gate.